C-1230   CAREER EXAMINATION SERIES

This is your
PASSBOOK for...

Custodial Worker

Test Preparation Study Guide
Questions & Answers

NLC®

NATIONAL LEARNING CORPORATION®

COPYRIGHT NOTICE

This book is SOLELY intended for, is sold ONLY to, and its use is RESTRICTED to individual, bona fide applicants or candidates who qualify by virtue of having seriously filed applications for appropriate license, certificate, professional and/or promotional advancement, higher school matriculation, scholarship, or other legitimate requirements of education and/or governmental authorities.

This book is NOT intended for use, class instruction, tutoring, training, duplication, copying, reprinting, excerption, or adaptation, etc., by:

1) Other publishers
2) Proprietors and/or Instructors of "Coaching" and/or Preparatory Courses
3) Personnel and/or Training Divisions of commercial, industrial, and governmental organizations
4) Schools, colleges, or universities and/or their departments and staffs, including teachers and other personnel
5) Testing Agencies or Bureaus
6) Study groups which seek by the purchase of a single volume to copy and/or duplicate and/or adapt this material for use by the group as a whole without having purchased individual volumes for each of the members of the group
7) Et al.

Such persons would be in violation of appropriate Federal and State statutes.

PROVISION OF LICENSING AGREEMENTS – Recognized educational, commercial, industrial, and governmental institutions and organizations, and others legitimately engaged in educational pursuits, including training, testing, and measurement activities, may address request for a licensing agreement to the copyright owners, who will determine whether, and under what conditions, including fees and charges, the materials in this book may be used them. In other words, a licensing facility exists for the legitimate use of the material in this book on other than an individual basis. However, it is asseverated and affirmed here that the material in this book CANNOT be used without the receipt of the express permission of such a licensing agreement from the Publishers. Inquiries re licensing should be addressed to the company, attention rights and permissions department.

All rights reserved, including the right of reproduction in whole or in part, in any form or by any means, electronic or mechanical, including photocopying, recording, or by any information storage and retrieval system, without permission in writing from the Publisher.

Copyright © 2024 by
National Learning Corporation

212 Michael Drive, Syosset, NY 11791
(516) 921-8888 • www.passbooks.com
E-mail: info@passbooks.com

PUBLISHED IN THE UNITED STATES OF AMERICA

PASSBOOK® SERIES

THE *PASSBOOK® SERIES* has been created to prepare applicants and candidates for the ultimate academic battlefield – the examination room.

At some time in our lives, each and every one of us may be required to take an examination – for validation, matriculation, admission, qualification, registration, certification, or licensure.

Based on the assumption that every applicant or candidate has met the basic formal educational standards, has taken the required number of courses, and read the necessary texts, the *PASSBOOK® SERIES* furnishes the one special preparation which may assure passing with confidence, instead of failing with insecurity. Examination questions – together with answers – are furnished as the basic vehicle for study so that the mysteries of the examination and its compounding difficulties may be eliminated or diminished by a sure method.

This book is meant to help you pass your examination provided that you qualify and are serious in your objective.

The entire field is reviewed through the huge store of content information which is succinctly presented through a provocative and challenging approach – the question-and-answer method.

A climate of success is established by furnishing the correct answers at the end of each test.

You soon learn to recognize types of questions, forms of questions, and patterns of questioning. You may even begin to anticipate expected outcomes.

You perceive that many questions are repeated or adapted so that you can gain acute insights, which may enable you to score many sure points.

You learn how to confront new questions, or types of questions, and to attack them confidently and work out the correct answers.

You note objectives and emphases, and recognize pitfalls and dangers, so that you may make positive educational adjustments.

Moreover, you are kept fully informed in relation to new concepts, methods, practices, and directions in the field.

You discover that you are actually taking the examination all the time: you are preparing for the examination by "taking" an examination, not by reading extraneous and/or supererogatory textbooks.

In short, this PASSBOOK®, used directedly, should be an important factor in helping you to pass your test.

CUSTODIAL WORKER

DUTIES

Works in a unit of custodial workers engaged in routine custodial care of public buildings and grounds; performs related duties as required.

Under direct supervision, the duties of this class involve the efficient and economical performance of building cleaning. Duties may involve the performance of maintenance activities and minor repair tasks. This work is performed according to a well-established routine. Supervision may be exercised over Laborers and/or Cleaners.

Custodial workers are responsible for keeping buildings in orderly, clean condition. They must complete cleaning duties, such as washing windows and walls, cleaning floors, shampooing rugs, picking up trash and restocking restrooms with supplies. They are also responsible for monitoring the building's security and safety by locking doors and checking electrical appliances to make sure they are working properly.

The duties required of a custodial worker include cleaning and polishing furniture and fixtures, cleaning laboratory equipment, mowing lawns, cleaning chimneys and setting up and arranging tables and chairs. He must also acquire supplies and equipment needed for cleaning, paint walls and move and lift heavy objects.

EXAMPLES OF WORK: (Illustrative Only)
- Sweeps, mops and waxes floors; washes walls and windows, dusts and performs other cleaning duties;
- Dusts desks, woodwork, furniture and other equipment;
- Cleans and mops lavatories and locker rooms and replaces soap or towels;
- Empties wastebaskets and collects and disposes of refuse;
- Moves and arranges chairs, tables and other furniture or equipment;
- Maintains cleanliness and sanitation of a swimming pool by checking temperature, chlorine levels, vacuuming;
- Assists with heavy work in kitchen and cafeteria;
- Checks windows and doors to see that they are closed and locked when proper;
- May make minor repairs to furniture, electrical fixtures, windows and shades, locks, faucets, heating system and other equipment;
- May undertake routine maintenance tasks related to building operating systems, i.e.; changing filters, etc.;
- May perform grounds keeping activities such as cleaning snow, mowing lawns, raking leaves, trimming shrubs, and general grounds maintenance such as clearing litter and debris;
- May act as monitor before and after school and in cafeteria;
- Performs a variety of errands and related custodial tasks.

SCOPE OF THE EXAMINATION
Written test designed to test for knowledge, skills, and/or abilities in such areas as:
1. Building cleaning;
2. Keeping simple inventory records; and
3. Ability read and follows written instructions.

HOW TO TAKE A TEST

I. YOU MUST PASS AN EXAMINATION

A. WHAT EVERY CANDIDATE SHOULD KNOW

Examination applicants often ask us for help in preparing for the written test. What can I study in advance? What kinds of questions will be asked? How will the test be given? How will the papers be graded?

As an applicant for a civil service examination, you may be wondering about some of these things. Our purpose here is to suggest effective methods of advance study and to describe civil service examinations.

Your chances for success on this examination can be increased if you know how to prepare. Those "pre-examination jitters" can be reduced if you know what to expect. You can even experience an adventure in good citizenship if you know why civil service exams are given.

B. WHY ARE CIVIL SERVICE EXAMINATIONS GIVEN?

Civil service examinations are important to you in two ways. As a citizen, you want public jobs filled by employees who know how to do their work. As a job seeker, you want a fair chance to compete for that job on an equal footing with other candidates. The best-known means of accomplishing this two-fold goal is the competitive examination.

Exams are widely publicized throughout the nation. They may be administered for jobs in federal, state, city, municipal, town or village governments or agencies.

Any citizen may apply, with some limitations, such as the age or residence of applicants. Your experience and education may be reviewed to see whether you meet the requirements for the particular examination. When these requirements exist, they are reasonable and applied consistently to all applicants. Thus, a competitive examination may cause you some uneasiness now, but it is your privilege and safeguard.

C. HOW ARE CIVIL SERVICE EXAMS DEVELOPED?

Examinations are carefully written by trained technicians who are specialists in the field known as "psychological measurement," in consultation with recognized authorities in the field of work that the test will cover. These experts recommend the subject matter areas or skills to be tested; only those knowledges or skills important to your success on the job are included. The most reliable books and source materials available are used as references. Together, the experts and technicians judge the difficulty level of the questions.

Test technicians know how to phrase questions so that the problem is clearly stated. Their ethics do not permit "trick" or "catch" questions. Questions may have been tried out on sample groups, or subjected to statistical analysis, to determine their usefulness.

Written tests are often used in combination with performance tests, ratings of training and experience, and oral interviews. All of these measures combine to form the best-known means of finding the right person for the right job.

II. HOW TO PASS THE WRITTEN TEST

A. NATURE OF THE EXAMINATION

To prepare intelligently for civil service examinations, you should know how they differ from school examinations you have taken. In school you were assigned certain definite pages to read or subjects to cover. The examination questions were quite detailed and usually emphasized memory. Civil service exams, on the other hand, try to discover your present ability to perform the duties of a position, plus your potentiality to learn these duties. In other words, a civil service exam attempts to predict how successful you will be. Questions cover such a broad area that they cannot be as minute and detailed as school exam questions.

In the public service similar kinds of work, or positions, are grouped together in one "class." This process is known as *position-classification*. All the positions in a class are paid according to the salary range for that class. One class title covers all of these positions, and they are all tested by the same examination.

B. FOUR BASIC STEPS

1) Study the announcement

How, then, can you know what subjects to study? Our best answer is: "Learn as much as possible about the class of positions for which you've applied." The exam will test the knowledge, skills and abilities needed to do the work.

Your most valuable source of information about the position you want is the official exam announcement. This announcement lists the training and experience qualifications. Check these standards and apply only if you come reasonably close to meeting them.

The brief description of the position in the examination announcement offers some clues to the subjects which will be tested. Think about the job itself. Review the duties in your mind. Can you perform them, or are there some in which you are rusty? Fill in the blank spots in your preparation.

Many jurisdictions preview the written test in the exam announcement by including a section called "Knowledge and Abilities Required," "Scope of the Examination," or some similar heading. Here you will find out specifically what fields will be tested.

2) Review your own background

Once you learn in general what the position is all about, and what you need to know to do the work, ask yourself which subjects you already know fairly well and which need improvement. You may wonder whether to concentrate on improving your strong areas or on building some background in your fields of weakness. When the announcement has specified "some knowledge" or "considerable knowledge," or has used adjectives like "beginning principles of..." or "advanced ... methods," you can get a clue as to the number and difficulty of questions to be asked in any given field. More questions, and hence broader coverage, would be included for those subjects which are more important in the work. Now weigh your strengths and weaknesses against the job requirements and prepare accordingly.

3) Determine the level of the position

Another way to tell how intensively you should prepare is to understand the level of the job for which you are applying. Is it the entering level? In other words, is this the position in which beginners in a field of work are hired? Or is it an intermediate or advanced level? Sometimes this is indicated by such words as "Junior" or "Senior" in the class title. Other jurisdictions use Roman numerals to designate the level – Clerk I, Clerk II, for example. The word "Supervisor" sometimes appears in the title. If the level is not indicated by the title, check the description of duties. Will you be working under very close supervision, or will you have responsibility for independent decisions in this work?

4) Choose appropriate study materials

Now that you know the subjects to be examined and the relative amount of each subject to be covered, you can choose suitable study materials. For beginning level jobs, or even advanced ones, if you have a pronounced weakness in some aspect of your training, read a modern, standard textbook in that field. Be sure it is up to date and has general coverage. Such books are normally available at your library, and the librarian will be glad to help you locate one. For entry-level positions, questions of appropriate difficulty are chosen – neither highly advanced questions, nor those too simple. Such questions require careful thought but not advanced training.

If the position for which you are applying is technical or advanced, you will read more advanced, specialized material. If you are already familiar with the basic principles of your field, elementary textbooks would waste your time. Concentrate on advanced textbooks and technical periodicals. Think through the concepts and review difficult problems in your field.

These are all general sources. You can get more ideas on your own initiative, following these leads. For example, training manuals and publications of the government agency which employs workers in your field can be useful, particularly for technical and professional positions. A letter or visit to the government department involved may result in more specific study suggestions, and certainly will provide you with a more definite idea of the exact nature of the position you are seeking.

III. KINDS OF TESTS

Tests are used for purposes other than measuring knowledge and ability to perform specified duties. For some positions, it is equally important to test ability to make adjustments to new situations or to profit from training. In others, basic mental abilities not dependent on information are essential. Questions which test these things may not appear as pertinent to the duties of the position as those which test for knowledge and information. Yet they are often highly important parts of a fair examination. For very general questions, it is almost impossible to help you direct your study efforts. What we can do is to point out some of the more common of these general abilities needed in public service positions and describe some typical questions.

1) General information

Broad, general information has been found useful for predicting job success in some kinds of work. This is tested in a variety of ways, from vocabulary lists to questions about current events. Basic background in some field of work, such as sociology or economics, may be sampled in a group of questions. Often these are principles which have become familiar to most persons through exposure rather than through formal training. It is difficult to advise you how to study for these questions; being alert to the world around you is our best suggestion.

2) Verbal ability

An example of an ability needed in many positions is verbal or language ability. Verbal ability is, in brief, the ability to use and understand words. Vocabulary and grammar tests are typical measures of this ability. Reading comprehension or paragraph interpretation questions are common in many kinds of civil service tests. You are given a paragraph of written material and asked to find its central meaning.

3) Numerical ability

Number skills can be tested by the familiar arithmetic problem, by checking paired lists of numbers to see which are alike and which are different, or by interpreting charts and graphs. In the latter test, a graph may be printed in the test booklet which you are asked to use as the basis for answering questions.

4) Observation

A popular test for law-enforcement positions is the observation test. A picture is shown to you for several minutes, then taken away. Questions about the picture test your ability to observe both details and larger elements.

5) Following directions

In many positions in the public service, the employee must be able to carry out written instructions dependably and accurately. You may be given a chart with several columns, each column listing a variety of information. The questions require you to carry out directions involving the information given in the chart.

6) Skills and aptitudes

Performance tests effectively measure some manual skills and aptitudes. When the skill is one in which you are trained, such as typing or shorthand, you can practice. These tests are often very much like those given in business school or high school courses. For many of the other skills and aptitudes, however, no short-time preparation can be made. Skills and abilities natural to you or that you have developed throughout your lifetime are being tested.

Many of the general questions just described provide all the data needed to answer the questions and ask you to use your reasoning ability to find the answers. Your best preparation for these tests, as well as for tests of facts and ideas, is to be at your physical and mental best. You, no doubt, have your own methods of getting into an exam-taking mood and keeping "in shape." The next section lists some ideas on this subject.

IV. KINDS OF QUESTIONS

Only rarely is the "essay" question, which you answer in narrative form, used in civil service tests. Civil service tests are usually of the short-answer type. Full instructions for answering these questions will be given to you at the examination. But in case this is your first experience with short-answer questions and separate answer sheets, here is what you need to know:

1) **Multiple-choice Questions**

Most popular of the short-answer questions is the "multiple choice" or "best answer" question. It can be used, for example, to test for factual knowledge, ability to solve problems or judgment in meeting situations found at work.

A multiple-choice question is normally one of three types—
- It can begin with an incomplete statement followed by several possible endings. You are to find the one ending which *best* completes the statement, although some of the others may not be entirely wrong.
- It can also be a complete statement in the form of a question which is answered by choosing one of the statements listed.

- It can be in the form of a problem – again you select the best answer.

Here is an example of a multiple-choice question with a discussion which should give you some clues as to the method for choosing the right answer:

When an employee has a complaint about his assignment, the action which will *best* help him overcome his difficulty is to
    A. discuss his difficulty with his coworkers
    B. take the problem to the head of the organization
    C. take the problem to the person who gave him the assignment
    D. say nothing to anyone about his complaint

In answering this question, you should study each of the choices to find which is best. Consider choice "A" – Certainly an employee may discuss his complaint with fellow employees, but no change or improvement can result, and the complaint remains unresolved. Choice "B" is a poor choice since the head of the organization probably does not know what assignment you have been given, and taking your problem to him is known as "going over the head" of the supervisor. The supervisor, or person who made the assignment, is the person who can clarify it or correct any injustice. Choice "C" is, therefore, correct. To say nothing, as in choice "D," is unwise. Supervisors have and interest in knowing the problems employees are facing, and the employee is seeking a solution to his problem.

2) True/False Questions

The "true/false" or "right/wrong" form of question is sometimes used. Here a complete statement is given. Your job is to decide whether the statement is right or wrong.

SAMPLE: A roaming cell-phone call to a nearby city costs less than a non-roaming call to a distant city.

This statement is wrong, or false, since roaming calls are more expensive.

This is not a complete list of all possible question forms, although most of the others are variations of these common types. You will always get complete directions for answering questions. Be sure you understand *how* to mark your answers – ask questions until you do.

V. RECORDING YOUR ANSWERS

Computer terminals are used more and more today for many different kinds of exams.
For an examination with very few applicants, you may be told to record your answers in the test booklet itself. Separate answer sheets are much more common. If this separate answer sheet is to be scored by machine – and this is often the case – it is highly important that you mark your answers correctly in order to get credit.
An electronic scoring machine is often used in civil service offices because of the speed with which papers can be scored. Machine-scored answer sheets must be marked with a pencil, which will be given to you. This pencil has a high graphite content which responds to the electronic scoring machine. As a matter of fact, stray dots may register as answers, so do not let your pencil rest on the answer sheet while you are pondering the correct answer. Also, if your pencil lead breaks or is otherwise defective, ask for another.

Since the answer sheet will be dropped in a slot in the scoring machine, be careful not to bend the corners or get the paper crumpled.

The answer sheet normally has five vertical columns of numbers, with 30 numbers to a column. These numbers correspond to the question numbers in your test booklet. After each number, going across the page are four or five pairs of dotted lines. These short dotted lines have small letters or numbers above them. The first two pairs may also have a "T" or "F" above the letters. This indicates that the first two pairs only are to be used if the questions are of the true-false type. If the questions are multiple choice, disregard the "T" and "F" and pay attention only to the small letters or numbers.

Answer your questions in the manner of the sample that follows:

32. The largest city in the United States is
    A. Washington, D.C.
    B. New York City
    C. Chicago
    D. Detroit
    E. San Francisco

1) Choose the answer you think is best. (New York City is the largest, so "B" is correct.)
2) Find the row of dotted lines numbered the same as the question you are answering. (Find row number 32)
3) Find the pair of dotted lines corresponding to the answer. (Find the pair of lines under the mark "B.")
4) Make a solid black mark between the dotted lines.

VI. BEFORE THE TEST

Common sense will help you find procedures to follow to get ready for an examination. Too many of us, however, overlook these sensible measures. Indeed, nervousness and fatigue have been found to be the most serious reasons why applicants fail to do their best on civil service tests. Here is a list of reminders:

- Begin your preparation early – Don't wait until the last minute to go scurrying around for books and materials or to find out what the position is all about.
- Prepare continuously – An hour a night for a week is better than an all-night cram session. This has been definitely established. What is more, a night a week for a month will return better dividends than crowding your study into a shorter period of time.
- Locate the place of the exam – You have been sent a notice telling you when and where to report for the examination. If the location is in a different town or otherwise unfamiliar to you, it would be well to inquire the best route and learn something about the building.
- Relax the night before the test – Allow your mind to rest. Do not study at all that night. Plan some mild recreation or diversion; then go to bed early and get a good night's sleep.
- Get up early enough to make a leisurely trip to the place for the test – This way unforeseen events, traffic snarls, unfamiliar buildings, etc. will not upset you.
- Dress comfortably – A written test is not a fashion show. You will be known by number and not by name, so wear something comfortable.

- Leave excess paraphernalia at home – Shopping bags and odd bundles will get in your way. You need bring only the items mentioned in the official notice you received; usually everything you need is provided. Do not bring reference books to the exam. They will only confuse those last minutes and be taken away from you when in the test room.
- Arrive somewhat ahead of time – If because of transportation schedules you must get there very early, bring a newspaper or magazine to take your mind off yourself while waiting.
- Locate the examination room – When you have found the proper room, you will be directed to the seat or part of the room where you will sit. Sometimes you are given a sheet of instructions to read while you are waiting. Do not fill out any forms until you are told to do so; just read them and be prepared.
- Relax and prepare to listen to the instructions
- If you have any physical problem that may keep you from doing your best, be sure to tell the test administrator. If you are sick or in poor health, you really cannot do your best on the exam. You can come back and take the test some other time.

VII. AT THE TEST

The day of the test is here and you have the test booklet in your hand. The temptation to get going is very strong. Caution! There is more to success than knowing the right answers. You must know how to identify your papers and understand variations in the type of short-answer question used in this particular examination. Follow these suggestions for maximum results from your efforts:

1) Cooperate with the monitor
The test administrator has a duty to create a situation in which you can be as much at ease as possible. He will give instructions, tell you when to begin, check to see that you are marking your answer sheet correctly, and so on. He is not there to guard you, although he will see that your competitors do not take unfair advantage. He wants to help you do your best.

2) Listen to all instructions
Don't jump the gun! Wait until you understand all directions. In most civil service tests you get more time than you need to answer the questions. So don't be in a hurry. Read each word of instructions until you clearly understand the meaning. Study the examples, listen to all announcements and follow directions. Ask questions if you do not understand what to do.

3) Identify your papers
Civil service exams are usually identified by number only. You will be assigned a number; you must not put your name on your test papers. Be sure to copy your number correctly. Since more than one exam may be given, copy your exact examination title.

4) Plan your time
Unless you are told that a test is a "speed" or "rate of work" test, speed itself is usually not important. Time enough to answer all the questions will be provided, but this does not mean that you have all day. An overall time limit has been set. Divide the total time (in minutes) by the number of questions to determine the approximate time you have for each question.

5) Do not linger over difficult questions

If you come across a difficult question, mark it with a paper clip (useful to have along) and come back to it when you have been through the booklet. One caution if you do this – be sure to skip a number on your answer sheet as well. Check often to be sure that you have not lost your place and that you are marking in the row numbered the same as the question you are answering.

6) Read the questions

Be sure you know what the question asks! Many capable people are unsuccessful because they failed to *read* the questions correctly.

7) Answer all questions

Unless you have been instructed that a penalty will be deducted for incorrect answers, it is better to guess than to omit a question.

8) Speed tests

It is often better NOT to guess on speed tests. It has been found that on timed tests people are tempted to spend the last few seconds before time is called in marking answers at random – without even reading them – in the hope of picking up a few extra points. To discourage this practice, the instructions may warn you that your score will be "corrected" for guessing. That is, a penalty will be applied. The incorrect answers will be deducted from the correct ones, or some other penalty formula will be used.

9) Review your answers

If you finish before time is called, go back to the questions you guessed or omitted to give them further thought. Review other answers if you have time.

10) Return your test materials

If you are ready to leave before others have finished or time is called, take ALL your materials to the monitor and leave quietly. Never take any test material with you. The monitor can discover whose papers are not complete, and taking a test booklet may be grounds for disqualification.

VIII. EXAMINATION TECHNIQUES

1) Read the general instructions carefully. These are usually printed on the first page of the exam booklet. As a rule, these instructions refer to the timing of the examination; the fact that you should not start work until the signal and must stop work at a signal, etc. If there are any *special* instructions, such as a choice of questions to be answered, make sure that you note this instruction carefully.

2) When you are ready to start work on the examination, that is as soon as the signal has been given, read the instructions to each question booklet, underline any key words or phrases, such as *least, best, outline, describe* and the like. In this way you will tend to answer as requested rather than discover on reviewing your paper that you *listed without describing*, that you selected the *worst* choice rather than the *best* choice, etc.

3) If the examination is of the objective or multiple-choice type – that is, each question will also give a series of possible answers: A, B, C or D, and you are called upon to select the best answer and write the letter next to that answer on your answer paper – it is advisable to start answering each question in turn. There may be anywhere from 50 to 100 such questions in the three or four hours allotted and you can see how much time would be taken if you read through all the questions before beginning to answer any. Furthermore, if you come across a question or group of questions which you know would be difficult to answer, it would undoubtedly affect your handling of all the other questions.

4) If the examination is of the essay type and contains but a few questions, it is a moot point as to whether you should read all the questions before starting to answer any one. Of course, if you are given a choice – say five out of seven and the like – then it is essential to read all the questions so you can eliminate the two that are most difficult. If, however, you are asked to answer all the questions, there may be danger in trying to answer the easiest one first because you may find that you will spend too much time on it. The best technique is to answer the first question, then proceed to the second, etc.

5) Time your answers. Before the exam begins, write down the time it started, then add the time allowed for the examination and write down the time it must be completed, then divide the time available somewhat as follows:
    - If 3-1/2 hours are allowed, that would be 210 minutes. If you have 80 objective-type questions, that would be an average of 2-1/2 minutes per question. Allow yourself no more than 2 minutes per question, or a total of 160 minutes, which will permit about 50 minutes to review.
    - If for the time allotment of 210 minutes there are 7 essay questions to answer, that would average about 30 minutes a question. Give yourself only 25 minutes per question so that you have about 35 minutes to review.

6) The most important instruction is to *read each question* and make sure you know what is wanted. The second most important instruction is to *time yourself properly* so that you answer every question. The third most important instruction is to *answer every question*. Guess if you have to but include something for each question. Remember that you will receive no credit for a blank and will probably receive some credit if you write something in answer to an essay question. If you guess a letter – say "B" for a multiple-choice question – you may have guessed right. If you leave a blank as an answer to a multiple-choice question, the examiners may respect your feelings but it will not add a point to your score. Some exams may penalize you for wrong answers, so in such cases *only*, you may not want to guess unless you have some basis for your answer.

7) Suggestions
    a. Objective-type questions
        1. Examine the question booklet for proper sequence of pages and questions
        2. Read all instructions carefully
        3. Skip any question which seems too difficult; return to it after all other questions have been answered
        4. Apportion your time properly; do not spend too much time on any single question or group of questions

5. Note and underline key words – *all, most, fewest, least, best, worst, same, opposite,* etc.
6. Pay particular attention to negatives
7. Note unusual option, e.g., unduly long, short, complex, different or similar in content to the body of the question
8. Observe the use of "hedging" words – *probably, may, most likely,* etc.
9. Make sure that your answer is put next to the same number as the question
10. Do not second-guess unless you have good reason to believe the second answer is definitely more correct
11. Cross out original answer if you decide another answer is more accurate; do not erase until you are ready to hand your paper in
12. Answer all questions; guess unless instructed otherwise
13. Leave time for review

  b. Essay questions
1. Read each question carefully
2. Determine exactly what is wanted. Underline key words or phrases.
3. Decide on outline or paragraph answer
4. Include many different points and elements unless asked to develop any one or two points or elements
5. Show impartiality by giving pros and cons unless directed to select one side only
6. Make and write down any assumptions you find necessary to answer the questions
7. Watch your English, grammar, punctuation and choice of words
8. Time your answers; don't crowd material

8) Answering the essay question

Most essay questions can be answered by framing the specific response around several key words or ideas. Here are a few such key words or ideas:

M's: manpower, materials, methods, money, management
P's: purpose, program, policy, plan, procedure, practice, problems, pitfalls, personnel, public relations

  a. Six basic steps in handling problems:
1. Preliminary plan and background development
2. Collect information, data and facts
3. Analyze and interpret information, data and facts
4. Analyze and develop solutions as well as make recommendations
5. Prepare report and sell recommendations
6. Install recommendations and follow up effectiveness

  b. Pitfalls to avoid
1. *Taking things for granted* – A statement of the situation does not necessarily imply that each of the elements is necessarily true; for example, a complaint may be invalid and biased so that all that can be taken for granted is that a complaint has been registered

2. *Considering only one side of a situation* – Wherever possible, indicate several alternatives and then point out the reasons you selected the best one
3. *Failing to indicate follow up* – Whenever your answer indicates action on your part, make certain that you will take proper follow-up action to see how successful your recommendations, procedures or actions turn out to be
4. *Taking too long in answering any single question* – Remember to time your answers properly

IX. AFTER THE TEST

Scoring procedures differ in detail among civil service jurisdictions although the general principles are the same. Whether the papers are hand-scored or graded by machine we have described, they are nearly always graded by number. That is, the person who marks the paper knows only the number – never the name – of the applicant. Not until all the papers have been graded will they be matched with names. If other tests, such as training and experience or oral interview ratings have been given, scores will be combined. Different parts of the examination usually have different weights. For example, the written test might count 60 percent of the final grade, and a rating of training and experience 40 percent. In many jurisdictions, veterans will have a certain number of points added to their grades.

After the final grade has been determined, the names are placed in grade order and an eligible list is established. There are various methods for resolving ties between those who get the same final grade – probably the most common is to place first the name of the person whose application was received first. Job offers are made from the eligible list in the order the names appear on it. You will be notified of your grade and your rank as soon as all these computations have been made. This will be done as rapidly as possible.

People who are found to meet the requirements in the announcement are called "eligibles." Their names are put on a list of eligible candidates. An eligible's chances of getting a job depend on how high he stands on this list and how fast agencies are filling jobs from the list.

When a job is to be filled from a list of eligibles, the agency asks for the names of people on the list of eligibles for that job. When the civil service commission receives this request, it sends to the agency the names of the three people highest on this list. Or, if the job to be filled has specialized requirements, the office sends the agency the names of the top three persons who meet these requirements from the general list.

The appointing officer makes a choice from among the three people whose names were sent to him. If the selected person accepts the appointment, the names of the others are put back on the list to be considered for future openings.

That is the rule in hiring from all kinds of eligible lists, whether they are for typist, carpenter, chemist, or something else. For every vacancy, the appointing officer has his choice of any one of the top three eligibles on the list. This explains why the person whose name is on top of the list sometimes does not get an appointment when some of the persons lower on the list do. If the appointing officer chooses the second or third eligible, the No. 1 eligible does not get a job at once, but stays on the list until he is appointed or the list is terminated.

X. HOW TO PASS THE INTERVIEW TEST

The examination for which you applied requires an oral interview test. You have already taken the written test and you are now being called for the interview test – the final part of the formal examination.

You may think that it is not possible to prepare for an interview test and that there are no procedures to follow during an interview. Our purpose is to point out some things you can do in advance that will help you and some good rules to follow and pitfalls to avoid while you are being interviewed.

What is an interview supposed to test?

The written examination is designed to test the technical knowledge and competence of the candidate; the oral is designed to evaluate intangible qualities, not readily measured otherwise, and to establish a list showing the relative fitness of each candidate – as measured against his competitors – for the position sought. Scoring is not on the basis of "right" and "wrong," but on a sliding scale of values ranging from "not passable" to "outstanding." As a matter of fact, it is possible to achieve a relatively low score without a single "incorrect" answer because of evident weakness in the qualities being measured.

Occasionally, an examination may consist entirely of an oral test – either an individual or a group oral. In such cases, information is sought concerning the technical knowledges and abilities of the candidate, since there has been no written examination for this purpose. More commonly, however, an oral test is used to supplement a written examination.

Who conducts interviews?

The composition of oral boards varies among different jurisdictions. In nearly all, a representative of the personnel department serves as chairman. One of the members of the board may be a representative of the department in which the candidate would work. In some cases, "outside experts" are used, and, frequently, a businessman or some other representative of the general public is asked to serve. Labor and management or other special groups may be represented. The aim is to secure the services of experts in the appropriate field.

However the board is composed, it is a good idea (and not at all improper or unethical) to ascertain in advance of the interview who the members are and what groups they represent. When you are introduced to them, you will have some idea of their backgrounds and interests, and at least you will not stutter and stammer over their names.

What should be done before the interview?

While knowledge about the board members is useful and takes some of the surprise element out of the interview, there is other preparation which is more substantive. It *is* possible to prepare for an oral interview – in several ways:

1) Keep a copy of your application and review it carefully before the interview

This may be the only document before the oral board, and the starting point of the interview. Know what education and experience you have listed there, and the sequence and dates of all of it. Sometimes the board will ask you to review the highlights of your experience for them; you should not have to hem and haw doing it.

2) Study the class specification and the examination announcement

Usually, the oral board has one or both of these to guide them. The qualities, characteristics or knowledges required by the position sought are stated in these documents. They offer valuable clues as to the nature of the oral interview. For example, if the job involves supervisory responsibilities, the announcement will usually indicate that knowledge of modern supervisory methods and the qualifications of the candidate as a supervisor will be tested. If so, you can expect such questions, frequently in the form of a hypothetical situation which you are expected to solve. NEVER go into an oral without knowledge of the duties and responsibilities of the job you seek.

3) Think through each qualification required

Try to visualize the kind of questions you would ask if you were a board member. How well could you answer them? Try especially to appraise your own knowledge and background in each area, *measured against the job sought*, and identify any areas in which you are weak. Be critical and realistic – do not flatter yourself.

4) Do some general reading in areas in which you feel you may be weak

For example, if the job involves supervision and your past experience has NOT, some general reading in supervisory methods and practices, particularly in the field of human relations, might be useful. Do NOT study agency procedures or detailed manuals. The oral board will be testing your understanding and capacity, not your memory.

5) Get a good night's sleep and watch your general health and mental attitude

You will want a clear head at the interview. Take care of a cold or any other minor ailment, and of course, no hangovers.

What should be done on the day of the interview?

Now comes the day of the interview itself. Give yourself plenty of time to get there. Plan to arrive somewhat ahead of the scheduled time, particularly if your appointment is in the fore part of the day. If a previous candidate fails to appear, the board might be ready for you a bit early. By early afternoon an oral board is almost invariably behind schedule if there are many candidates, and you may have to wait. Take along a book or magazine to read, or your application to review, but leave any extraneous material in the waiting room when you go in for your interview. In any event, relax and compose yourself.

The matter of dress is important. The board is forming impressions about you – from your experience, your manners, your attitude, and your appearance. Give your personal appearance careful attention. Dress your best, but not your flashiest. Choose conservative, appropriate clothing, and be sure it is immaculate. This is a business interview, and your appearance should indicate that you regard it as such. Besides, being well groomed and properly dressed will help boost your confidence.

Sooner or later, someone will call your name and escort you into the interview room. *This is it.* From here on you are on your own. It is too late for any more preparation. But remember, you asked for this opportunity to prove your fitness, and you are here because your request was granted.

What happens when you go in?

The usual sequence of events will be as follows: The clerk (who is often the board stenographer) will introduce you to the chairman of the oral board, who will introduce you to the other members of the board. Acknowledge the introductions before you sit down. Do not be surprised if you find a microphone facing you or a stenotypist sitting by. Oral interviews are usually recorded in the event of an appeal or other review.

Usually the chairman of the board will open the interview by reviewing the highlights of your education and work experience from your application – primarily for the benefit of the other members of the board, as well as to get the material into the record. Do not interrupt or comment unless there is an error or significant misinterpretation; if that is the case, do not hesitate. But do not quibble about insignificant matters. Also, he will usually ask you some question about your education, experience or your present job – partly to get you to start talking and to establish the interviewing "rapport." He may start the actual questioning, or turn it over to one of the other members. Frequently, each member undertakes the questioning on a particular area, one in which he is perhaps most competent, so you can expect each member to participate in the examination. Because time is limited, you may also expect some rather abrupt switches in the direction the questioning takes, so do not be upset by it. Normally, a board member will not pursue a single line of questioning unless he discovers a particular strength or weakness.

After each member has participated, the chairman will usually ask whether any member has any further questions, then will ask you if you have anything you wish to add. Unless you are expecting this question, it may floor you. Worse, it may start you off on an extended, extemporaneous speech. The board is not usually seeking more information. The question is principally to offer you a last opportunity to present further qualifications or to indicate that you have nothing to add. So, if you feel that a significant qualification or characteristic has been overlooked, it is proper to point it out in a sentence or so. Do not compliment the board on the thoroughness of their examination – they have been sketchy, and you know it. If you wish, merely say, "No thank you, I have nothing further to add." This is a point where you can "talk yourself out" of a good impression or fail to present an important bit of information. Remember, *you close the interview yourself.*

The chairman will then say, "That is all, Mr. _____, thank you." Do not be startled; the interview is over, and quicker than you think. Thank him, gather your belongings and take your leave. Save your sigh of relief for the other side of the door.

How to put your best foot forward

Throughout this entire process, you may feel that the board individually and collectively is trying to pierce your defenses, seek out your hidden weaknesses and embarrass and confuse you. Actually, this is not true. They are obliged to make an appraisal of your qualifications for the job you are seeking, and they want to see you in your best light. Remember, they must interview all candidates and a non-cooperative candidate may become a failure in spite of their best efforts to bring out his qualifications. Here are 15 suggestions that will help you:

1) Be natural – Keep your attitude confident, not cocky

If you are not confident that you can do the job, do not expect the board to be. Do not apologize for your weaknesses, try to bring out your strong points. The board is interested in a positive, not negative, presentation. Cockiness will antagonize any board member and make him wonder if you are covering up a weakness by a false show of strength.

2) Get comfortable, but don't lounge or sprawl

Sit erectly but not stiffly. A careless posture may lead the board to conclude that you are careless in other things, or at least that you are not impressed by the importance of the occasion. Either conclusion is natural, even if incorrect. Do not fuss with your clothing, a pencil or an ashtray. Your hands may occasionally be useful to emphasize a point; do not let them become a point of distraction.

3) Do not wisecrack or make small talk

This is a serious situation, and your attitude should show that you consider it as such. Further, the time of the board is limited – they do not want to waste it, and neither should you.

4) Do not exaggerate your experience or abilities

In the first place, from information in the application or other interviews and sources, the board may know more about you than you think. Secondly, you probably will not get away with it. An experienced board is rather adept at spotting such a situation, so do not take the chance.

5) If you know a board member, do not make a point of it, yet do not hide it

Certainly you are not fooling him, and probably not the other members of the board. Do not try to take advantage of your acquaintanceship – it will probably do you little good.

6) Do not dominate the interview

Let the board do that. They will give you the clues – do not assume that you have to do all the talking. Realize that the board has a number of questions to ask you, and do not try to take up all the interview time by showing off your extensive knowledge of the answer to the first one.

7) Be attentive

You only have 20 minutes or so, and you should keep your attention at its sharpest throughout. When a member is addressing a problem or question to you, give him your undivided attention. Address your reply principally to him, but do not exclude the other board members.

8) Do not interrupt

A board member may be stating a problem for you to analyze. He will ask you a question when the time comes. Let him state the problem, and wait for the question.

9) Make sure you understand the question

Do not try to answer until you are sure what the question is. If it is not clear, restate it in your own words or ask the board member to clarify it for you. However, do not haggle about minor elements.

10) Reply promptly but not hastily

A common entry on oral board rating sheets is "candidate responded readily," or "candidate hesitated in replies." Respond as promptly and quickly as you can, but do not jump to a hasty, ill-considered answer.

11) Do not be peremptory in your answers

A brief answer is proper – but do not fire your answer back. That is a losing game from your point of view. The board member can probably ask questions much faster than you can answer them.

12) Do not try to create the answer you think the board member wants

He is interested in what kind of mind you have and how it works – not in playing games. Furthermore, he can usually spot this practice and will actually grade you down on it.

13) Do not switch sides in your reply merely to agree with a board member

Frequently, a member will take a contrary position merely to draw you out and to see if you are willing and able to defend your point of view. Do not start a debate, yet do not surrender a good position. If a position is worth taking, it is worth defending.

14) Do not be afraid to admit an error in judgment if you are shown to be wrong

The board knows that you are forced to reply without any opportunity for careful consideration. Your answer may be demonstrably wrong. If so, admit it and get on with the interview.

15) Do not dwell at length on your present job

The opening question may relate to your present assignment. Answer the question but do not go into an extended discussion. You are being examined for a *new* job, not your present one. As a matter of fact, try to phrase ALL your answers in terms of the job for which you are being examined.

Basis of Rating

Probably you will forget most of these "do's" and "don'ts" when you walk into the oral interview room. Even remembering them all will not ensure you a passing grade. Perhaps you did not have the qualifications in the first place. But remembering them will help you to put your best foot forward, without treading on the toes of the board members.

Rumor and popular opinion to the contrary notwithstanding, an oral board wants you to make the best appearance possible. They know you are under pressure – but they also want to see how you respond to it as a guide to what your reaction would be under the pressures of the job you seek. They will be influenced by the degree of poise you display, the personal traits you show and the manner in which you respond.

ABOUT THIS BOOK

This book contains tests divided into Examination Sections. Go through each test, answering every question in the margin. We have also attached a sample answer sheet at the back of the book that can be removed and used. At the end of each test look at the answer key and check your answers. On the ones you got wrong, look at the right answer choice and learn. Do not fill in the answers first. Do not memorize the questions and answers, but understand the answer and principles involved. On your test, the questions will likely be different from the samples. Questions are changed and new ones added. If you understand these past questions you should have success with any changes that arise. Tests may consist of several types of questions. We have additional books on each subject should more study be advisable or necessary for you. Finally, the more you study, the better prepared you will be. This book is intended to be the last thing you study before you walk into the examination room. Prior study of relevant texts is also recommended. NLC publishes some of these in our Fundamental Series. Knowledge and good sense are important factors in passing your exam. Good luck also helps. So now study this Passbook, absorb the material contained within and take that knowledge into the examination. Then do your best to pass that exam.

EXAMINATION SECTION

EXAMINATION SECTION
TEST 1

DIRECTIONS: Each question or incomplete statement is followed by several suggested answers or completions. Select the one that BEST answers the question or completes the statement. *PRINT THE LETTER OF THE CORRECT ANSWER IN THE SPACE AT THE RIGHT.*

1. Of the following, the FIRST thing a custodian should do when he enters the boiler room to check on the operation of the boiler is to   1.____

    A. check the boiler water level
    B. blow down the boiler
    C. check the boiler water temperature
    D. check the fuel supply

2. Cleaners will usually be motivated to do a GOOD job by a custodian who   2.____

    A. lets them get away with poor performance
    B. treats them fairly
    C. treats some of them more favorably than others
    D. lets them take a nap in the afternoon

3. The MOST important aim of a training program in fire prevention is to train the custodial staff to   3.____

    A. be constantly alert to fire hazards
    B. assist the city fire department in extinguishing fires
    C. maintain the sprinkler system
    D. climb ladders safely

4. The one of the following which is NOT recommended for prolonging the useful life of a hair broom is to   4.____

    A. rotate the brush to avoid wear on one side only
    B. wash the brush by using it as a mop once a week
    C. comb the brush weekly
    D. hang the brush in storage to avoid resting on the bristles

5. A GOOD indication of the quality of the cleaning operation in a building is the   5.____

    A. amount of cleaning material used each month
    B. number of cleaners employed
    C. number of complaints of unsanitary conditions received
    D. number of square feet of hall space cleaned daily

6. Spontaneous ignition is MOST likely to occur in a   6.____

    A. pile of oily rags
    B. vented fuel oil tank
    C. metal file cabinet filled with papers in file folders
    D. covered metal container containing clean rags

7. A boiler test kit is used to test

   A. boiler water
   C. pressure gauges
   B. fuel oil
   D. steam consumption

8. The MOST common cause of a dripping faucet is a

   A. broken stem
   B. cracked bonnet
   C. worn washer
   D. loose retaining screw on the handle

9. The lighting systems in public buildings usually operate MOST NEARLY on _____ volts.

   A. 6
   B. 24
   C. 115
   D. 220

10. A type of hammer which can be used to remove nails from wood is the

    A. ball-peen
    B. mallet
    C. sledge
    D. claw

11. A vacuum pump is used in a(n) _____ heating system.

    A. steam
    C. hot water
    B. hot air
    D. electric

12. An expansion tank is used in a(n) heating system.

    A. steam
    C. hot water
    B. hot air
    D. electric

13. The thermostat in the office area of a public building should have a winter daytime setting of about _____ ° F.

    A. 50
    B. 60
    C. 70
    D. 80

14. The fuel oil which USUALLY requires preheating before it enters an oil burner is known as

    A. #1
    B. #2
    C. #4
    D. #6

15. The domestic hot water in a large public building is circulated by

    A. gravity flow
    B. a pump which runs continuously
    C. a pump which is controlled by water pressure
    D. a pump which is controlled by water temperature

16. The vaporstat on a rotary-cup boil burner senses

    A. oil temperature
    C. secondary air pressure
    B. primary air pressure
    D. oil pressure

17. The emergency switch for a fully automatic oil burner is USUALLY located

    A. at the entrance to the boiler room
    B. on the burner
    C. at the electrical distribution panel in the boiler room
    D. at the electric service meter panel

18. The try-cocks on a steam boiler are used to 18.____

    A. drain the boiler
    B. check the operation of the safety valves
    C. check the water level in the boiler
    D. drain the pressure gauge

19. The draft in a natural draft furnace is USUALLY measured in 19.____

    A. pounds   B. inches of mercury
    C. inches of water   D. cubic feet

20. The stack temperature in a low pressure oil-fired steam boiler installation should be 20.____
    about _____ ° F.

    A. 212   B. 275   C. 350   D. 875

21. A material that transmits heat VERY POORLY is a good 21.____

    A. insulator   B. conductor
    C. radiator   D. convector

22. The asbestos covering on steam lines 22.____

    A. increases the flow of steam
    B. reduces the loss of heat
    C. increases the loss of heat
    D. prevents leaks

23. The air in a closed room that is heated by a radiator USUALLY 23.____

    A. settles to the floor   B. rises
    C. remains stationary   D. contracts

24. A gallon of water which is changed to steam at atmosphere pressure will increase in volume about _____ times. 24.____

    A. 5   B. 15   C. 150   D. 1500

25. The humidity of the air means its 25.____

    A. clarity   B. weight
    C. dust content   D. moisture content

26. The safety device which opens automatically to release excessive steam pressure in a 26.____
    boiler is the _____ valve.

    A. check   B. safety
    C. gate   D. quick opening

27. Of the following devices, the one which is NOT usually found on a natural draft coal-fired 27.____
    boiler is the

    A. feedwater regulator   B. low-water cutout
    C. safety valve   D. water column

28. The number of degree days for two days in the city when the temperature for these two days averages 55° F is

    A. 2   B. 10   C. 20   D. 30

29. A detergent is GENERALLY used in

    A. waterproofing walls
    B. killing crabgrass
    C. cleaning floor and walls
    D. exterminating rodents

30. The MAIN reason for using a sweeping compound is to

    A. spot-finish waxed surfaces
    B. retard dust when sweeping floors
    C. loosen accumulations of grease
    D. remove paint spots from tile flooring

31. The one of the following cleaning agents which is RECOMMENDED for use on marble floors is

    A. an acid cleaner
    B. a soft soap
    C. trisodium phosphate
    D. a neutral liquid detergent

32. A cleaning solution of one cup of soap chips dissolved in a pail of warm water can be used to wash

    A. painted walls   B. rubber tile
    C. marble walls   D. terrazzo floors

33. Sodium fluoride is a

    A. pesticide   B. disinfectant
    C. detergent   D. paint thinner

34. Scratches or burns in linoleum, rubber tile, or cork floors should be removed by rubbing with

    A. crocus cloth   B. fine steel wool
    C. sandpaper   D. emery cloth

35. A room 12 feet wide by 25 feet long has a floor area of _____ square feet.

    A. 37   B. 200   C. 300   D. 400

36. A cleaning solution should be applied to a painted wall using a

    A. wool rag   B. brush   C. sponge   D. squeegee

37. When scrubbing a wooden floor, it is advisable to
    A. flood the surface with the cleaning solution in order to float the dirt out of all cracks and crevices
    B. hose off the loosened dirt before starting the scrubbing operation
    C. pick up the cleaning solution as soon as possible
    D. mix a mild acid with the cleaning solution in order to clean the surface quickly

37.____

38. How many hours will it take a worker to sweep a floor space of 2800 square feet if he sweeps at the rate of 800 square feet per hour?
    A. 8   B. 6 1/2   C. 3 1/2   D. 2 1/2

38.____

39. One gallon of water contains
    A. 2 quarts   B. 4 quarts   C. 2 pints   D. 4 pints

39.____

40. A standard cleaning solution is prepared by mixing 4 ounces of detergent powder in 2 gallons of water.
    The number of ounces of detergent powder needed, for the same strength solution, in 5 gallons of water is
    A. 4   B. 6   C. 8   D. 10

40.____

KEY (CORRECT ANSWERS)

1.	A	11.	A	21.	A	31.	D
2.	B	12.	C	22.	B	32.	A
3.	A	13.	C	23.	B	33.	A
4.	B	14.	D	24.	D	34.	B
5.	C	15.	D	25.	D	35.	C
6.	A	16.	B	26.	B	36.	C
7.	A	17.	A	27.	B	37.	C
8.	C	18.	C	28.	C	38.	C
9.	C	19.	C	29.	C	39.	B
10.	D	20.	C	30.	B	40.	D

TEST 2

DIRECTIONS: Each question or incomplete statement is followed by several suggested answers or completions. Select the one that BEST answers the question or completes the statement. *PRINT THE LETTER OF THE CORRECT ANSWER IN THE SPACE AT THE RIGHT.*

1. A custodian should know approximately how long it takes to do each job so that he can   1.___
   A. judge correctly if the person doing the job is working too slowly
   B. tell how much time to take if he has to do it himself
   C. retrain experienced employees in better work habits
   D. tell how much time to dock a worker if he skips that part of the work

2. In order to have building employees willing to follow standardized cleaning procedures, the custodian must be prepared to   2.___
   A. demonstrate the advantages of the procedures
   B. do part of the cleaning work each day until the employees learn the procedures
   C. let the employees go home early if they save time using the procedures
   D. offer incentive pay to encourage their use

3. The BEST agent to use to remove chewing gum from fabric is   3.___
   A. ammonia   B. chlorine bleach
   C. a degreaser   D. water

4. Water emulsion wax should NOT be used on   4.___
   A. linoleum   B. cork tile flooring
   C. furniture   D. rubber tile flooring

5. Tops of desks, file cabinets, and bookcases are BEST dusted with a   5.___
   A. damp cloth   B. treated cotton cloth
   C. damp sponge   D. feather duster

6. The one of the following which is NOT a material used in scrub brushes is   6.___
   A. tampico   B. terrazzo   C. palmetto   D. bassine

7. A chamois is PROPERLY used to   7.___
   A. wash enamel surfaces   B. wash window glass
   C. dry enamel surfaces   D. dry window glass

8. The PROPER sequence of operations used in cleaning an office, when the floor is to be swept with a broom, is   8.___
   A. clean ashtrays, empty wastebaskets, sweep, dust
   B. sweep, dust, clean ashtrays, empty wastebaskets
   C. dust, sweep, clean ashtrays, empty wastebaskets
   D. clean ashtrays, empty wastebaskets, dust, sweep

9. Of the following, the MOST common result of accidents occurring while using hand tools is

    A. loss of limbs
    B. loss of eyesight
    C. infection of wounds
    D. loss of life

10. A twenty-four foot long extension ladder is placed with its top resting against a vertical wall.
    The SAFEST procedure would be to place the base of the ladder a distance from the wall of _____ feet.

    A. 3   B. 6   C. 9   D. 12

11. The one of the following extinguishing agents which should NOT be used on an oil fire is

    A. foam
    B. sand
    C. water
    D. carbon dioxide

12. The extinguishing agent in a portable soda-acid fire extinguisher is

    A. sodium bicarbonate
    B. sulphuric acid
    C. carbon dioxide
    D. water

13. The information on an accident report which is MOST useful toward prevention of similar accidents is the

    A. name of the victim
    B. cause of the accident
    C. type of injury sustained
    D. date of the accident

14. A fusible link is used to

    A. weld two pieces of chain together
    B. solder an electric wire to a terminal
    C. attach a ground wire to a water pipe
    D. hold a fire door open

15. When making up a pipe joint in the shop, between a nipple and a valve, the _____ should be held in a _____ vise and the _____ .

    A. valve; square-jawed; pipe screwed into it
    B. pipe; square-jawed; valve screwed onto it
    C. valve; pipe; pipe screwed into it
    D. pipe; pipe; valve screwed onto it

16. A city water meter is USUALLY read in

    A. pounds
    B. cubic feet
    C. pounds per square inch
    D. degrees

17. The valve which AUTOMATICALLY prevents back flow in a water pipe is called a _____ valve.

    A. check   B. globe   C. gate   D. by-pass

18. The BEST wrench to use to tighten a galvanized iron pipe valve or fitting which has hexagonal ends is _____ wrench.

    A. stillson   B. strap   C. monkey   D. socket

19. A flushometer would be connected to a

    A. water meter   B. toilet bowl
    C. garden hose   D. fire hose

20. Electric service meters are read in

    A. kilowatt hours   B. electrons
    C. amperes   D. volts

21. The device used to reduce the voltage of an electric circuit is the

    A. voltmeter   B. fuse
    C. circuit breaker   D. transformer

22. Ordinary light bulbs are USUALLY rated in

    A. watts   B. ohms   C. amperes   D. filaments

23. The electric plug on a scrubbing machine should be plugged into a

    A. light socket   B. wall outlet
    C. fuse receptacle   D. dimmer switch

24. The device which should be used to connect the output shaft of an electric motor to the input shaft of the centrifugal pump is the

    A. flexible coupling   B. petcock
    C. alemite fitting   D. clutch

25. The type of wood screw which is used to attach a hinge to a door jamb is the _____ screw.

    A. flat head   B. lag
    C. round head   D. square head

26. Of the following bolt sizes, the one which identifies the bolt that has the LARGEST diameter is

    A. 4 - 40   B. 6 - 32   C. 8 - 32   D. 10 - 24

27. The tool MOST commonly used with a mitre box to cut wooden molding is the _____ saw.

    A. hack   B. rip   C. keyhole   D. back

28. The type of lock which can be opened ONLY from the lock side of a door is the

    A. cylinder lock   B. spring latch
    C. padlock   D. mortise lock

29. A key which will open many locks of the same type is USUALLY called a _____ key.

    A. tumbler   B. master   C. magnetic   D. cotter

30. Of the following, the BEST lubricant to use on locks is

    A. grease
    B. graphite
    C. mineral oil
    D. talc

31. A device which allows an exit door to be opened from the inside by pressing on a horizontal bar is known as a

    A. door pull
    B. double bolt bar lock
    C. cross bolt dead lock
    D. panic bolt

32. The MOST useful information for preventing future vandalism which should be included in a vandalism report is

    A. a list of damaged items
    B. how the vandals got into the building
    C. a list of stolen items
    D. how many hours it took to clean up the mess

33. A custodian should tour his assigned building a short time after the closing time MAINLY to see that

    A. any office workers who are on overtime are really working
    B. no unauthorized persons are in the building
    C. all the hall lights are turned off
    D. all the typewriters have dust covers on

34. As a custodian, if you want to be sure that a worker understands some difficult job instructions you just gave him, it is MOST important for you to

    A. ask him questions about the instructions
    B. ask him to write the instructions down and show them to you
    C. ask an experienced man to check on his work
    D. check on his work yourself after he has finished

35. The BEST way for a custodian to keep control of his work assignments is to

    A. inspect the building weekly
    B. make a written schedule and check it against the work being done each day
    C. have the men report to him at the completion of each job and then give them a new assignment
    D. leave the men on their own until complaints are received

36. The MOST important thing a custodian must do is to

    A. plan ahead
    B. keep stock records
    C. put out the lights when leaving the building
    D. answer the telephone

37. One of the ways in which a custodian can maintain proper control of his subordinates is to

    A. punish every minor infraction of the rules
    B. deny making any mistakes himself

C. criticize his own supervisor to show his own superiority
D. instill the idea that he keeps an eye on everything in his department

38. You see that one of your workers is not doing a job according to the safety rules. You should

   A. correct him so that he will know how to work
   B. take him off the job and send him to training class
   C. let it go and wait to see if he works this way all the time
   D. bawl him out

39. The BEST action a custodian can take to promote the security of his building is to

   A. depend on the police department to constantly patrol the area
   B. turn out all outside lights so that it will be difficult for intruders to find entry at night
   C. be sure all doors and windows are locked securely before the last person leaves the building at night
   D. allow only employees to enter the building during the day

40. The one thing a custodian should NOT do after his building has been broken into is to

   A. notify the police
   B. report the incident to his supervisor
   C. leave the damage to doors or windows unrepaired until his supervisor can inspect them on his regularly scheduled visit
   D. make the point of entry more secure than it was before the break-in

---

KEY (CORRECT ANSWERS)

1. A	11. C	21. D	31. D
2. A	12. D	22. A	32. B
3. C	13. B	23. B	33. B
4. C	14. D	24. A	34. A
5. B	15. D	25. A	35. B
6. B	16. B	26. D	36. A
7. D	17. A	27. D	37. D
8. A	18. C	28. C	38. A
9. C	19. B	29. B	39. C
10. B	20. A	30. B	40. C

EXAMINATION SECTION
TEST 1

DIRECTIONS: Each question or incomplete statement is followed by several suggested answers or completions. Select the one that BEST answers the question or completes the statement. *PRINT THE LETTER OF THE CORRECT ANSWER IN THE SPACE AT THE RIGHT.*

1. The KEY figure in any custodial safety program is the 1.____
   A. custodian   B. cleaner   C. mayor   D. commissioner

2. A custodian must inspect or have a maintenance man inspect every window cleaner's safety belt AT LEAST 2.____
   A. each time the windows are washed
   B. once a month
   C. once a year
   D. once every second year

3. A custodian's written instruction to his staff on the subject of security in public buildings should include instructions to 3.____
   A. exclude the public at all times
   B. admit the public at all times
   C. admit the public only if they are neat and well-dressed
   D. admit the public during specified hours

4. A custodian in charge of a building who is normally on duty during the daytime hours in a building which is cleaned at night should 4.____
   A. never make night inspections since he is not responsible for the cleanliness of the building
   B. make night inspections at least once a year
   C. never make night inspections because the cleaners will think he is spying on them
   D. make night inspections at least twice a month

5. The employee MOST likely to find the nests and runways in a building of roaches and vermin is a 5.____
   A. maintenance man   B. building custodian
   C. night cleaner   D. stationary fireman

6. When mopping, the pails containing the cleaning solutions should be 6.____
   A. slid along the floor to avoid injury due to lifting
   B. kept off the floor, preferably on a rolling platform
   C. shifted from place to place using a mop
   D. equipped with a spigot for applying the mopping solution

7. Of the following, the item that is considered a concrete floor sealer is
   A. water wax
   B. sodium hypochlorite
   C. sodium silicate
   D. linseed oil

8. A material COMMONLY used in detergent is
   A. rock salt
   B. Glauber's salt
   C. tri-sodium phosphate
   D. monosodium glutamate

9. A disinfectant material is one that will
   A. kill germs
   B. dissolve soil and stop odors
   C. give a clean odor and cover a disagreeable odor
   D. prevent soil buildup

10. When scrubbing a wooden floor, it is ADVISABLE to
    A. flood the surface with the cleaning solution in order to float the soil out of all crevices
    B. hose off the loosened soil before starting the scrubbing operation
    C. pick up the used solution as soon as possible
    D. mix a mild acid with the cleaning solution in order to clean the surface quickly

11. Before starting a wall washing operation, it is BEST to
    A. check the temperature of the water
    B. soak the sponge to be used
    C. check the pH of the mixed cleaning solution
    D. dust the wall to be washed

12. Of the following, the MOST nearly correct statement regarding the economical operation of the heating system in a building is that
    A. the heat should always be shut down at 4 P.M. and turned on at 8 A.M.
    B. the heat should be shut down only over the weekend
    C. it is best to keep the heat on at all times so that the number of complaints are kept to a minimum
    D. the times at which the heat is shut down and turned on should be varied depending on the prevailing outdoor temperature

13. A floor made of marble or granite chis imbedded in cement is USUALLY called
    A. terrazzo   B. linoleum   C. palmetto   D. parquet

14. In a 4-wire, 3-phase electrical supply system, the voltage between one phase and ground used for the lighting is MOST NEARLY
    A. 440   B. 230   C. 208   D. 115

15. Of the following, the one that takes the place of a fuse in an electrical circuit is a
    A. transformer
    B. circuit breaker
    C. condenser
    D. knife switch

16. Gas bills are USUALLY computed on the basis of
    A. cubic feet   B. gallons   C. pounds   D. kilowatts

17. An operating oil-fired steam boiler explosion may sometimes be caused by
    A. carrying too high a water level in the boiler
    B. inadequate purging of combustion chamber between fires
    C. overfiring the boiler
    D. carrying too high an oil temperature

18. The one of the following commercial sizes of anthracite which is the LARGEST in size is
    A. stove   B. chestnut   C. pea   D. rice

19. Assume that six windows of a public building facing one street have been consistently broken by boys playing ball after hours and over weekends.
    The BEST solution to this problem is to
    A. post a no ball playing sign on the wall
    B. erect protective screening outside the six windows
    C. post a guard on weekend patrol duty
    D. request special weekend police protection for the property

20. The BEST method or tool to use for cleaning dust from an unplastered cinder-block wall is
    A. a Tampico brush with stock cleaning solution
    B. a vacuum cleaner
    C. water under pressure from hose and nozzle
    D. a feather duster

21. Of the following, the LARGEST individual item of expense in operating a public building is generally the cost of
    A. cleaning   B. heating fuel
    C. electricity   D. elevator service

22. The CHIEF purpose for changing the handle of a floor brush from one side of the brush block to the other side is to
    A. allow the janitor to change hands
    B. make both sides of the brush equally dirty
    C. give both sides of the brush equal wear
    D. change the angle of sweeping

23. Of the following, the weight of mop MOST likely used in the nightly mopping of corridors, halls, or lobbies is _____ ounce.
    A. 8   B. 16   C. 24   D. 50

24. After sweeping assignment is completed, floor brushes should be stored
    A. in a pan of water
    B. by hanging the brushes on pegs or nails
    C. by piling the brushes on each other carefully
    D. in a normal sweeping position, bristles resting on the floor

25. Nylon-treated scrubbing discs
    A. require more water than scrubbing brushes
    B. require more detergent solution than scrubbing brushes
    C. must be used with cold water only
    D. are generally more effective than steel wool pads

26. Of the following, the BEST material to use to clean exterior bronze is
    A. pumice   B. paste wax
    C. wire wheel on portable buffer   D. lemon oil polish

27. The use of trisodium phosphate in cleaning polished marble should be AVOIDED because it
    A. may cause spalling
    B. discolors the surface of the marble
    C. builds up a slick surface on the marble
    D. pits the glazed surface and bleaches the marble

28. The floor area, in square feet, on which a properly treated dustless sweeping cloth can be used before the cloth must be washed is
    A. 500-1000   B. 2000-3000   C. 4000-6000   D. 8000-10000

29. A cleaning woman working a six-hour shift should be able to cover (clean) _____ Gilbert work units.
    A. 100-200   B. 400-500   C. 1100-1200   D. 6000-7000

30. An incipient fire is one which
    A. has just started and can be readily extinguished using an ordinary hand extinguisher
    B. occurs only in motor vehicles
    C. is burning out of control in a storeroom
    D. is a banked coal fire

31. Maintaining room temperature at 75°F in the winter time will increase fuel consumption above the amount needed to maintain 70°F by APPROXIMATELY
    A. 5%   B. 10%   C. 15%   D. 20%

32. Of the following, the one which represents the BEST practical combustion condition in an oil-fired low pressure steam plant is _____ stack temperature.
    A. 8% CO_2 - 500°F   B. 13% CO_2 - 400°F
    C. 10% CO_2 - 700°F   D. 6% CO_2 - 400°F

33. An office has floor dimensions of 6 ft. 6 in. wide by 22 ft. 0 in. long. The floor area of this office, in square feet, is MOST NEARLY
    A. 143   B. 263   C. 363   D. 463

34. Dollies are USUALLY used
    A. as convenient platforms upon which to store items
    B. as ornamental protective covers

C. to raise items to the required level
D. to transport items from one place to another

35. When lifting a heavy object from a table, which of the following rules is it MOST important to observe?
    A. Do not bend your knees.
    B. Do not stand too close to the object.
    C. Keep your back straight.
    D. Keep your shoulder level with the object

36. The FIRST objective of all fire prevention is
    A. confining fire to a limited area
    B. safeguarding life against fire
    C. reducing insurance rates
    D. preventing property damage

37. A custodian should know the equipment used in his work well enough to
    A. make any repairs which might be needed
    B. know what parts to remove in case of breakdown
    C. anticipate any reasonable possibility of a breakdown
    D. know all the lubricants specified by the manufacturer

38. The PRIMARY responsibility of a supervising custodian is to
    A. make friends of all subordinates
    B. search for new methods of doing the work
    C. win the respect of his superior
    D. get the work done properly within a reasonable time

39. When a custodian believes that the work of a subordinate is below standard, he should
    A. assign the employee to work that is considered undesirable
    B. do nothing immediately in the hope that the employee will bring his work up to standard without any help from the supervisor
    C. reduce the privileges of the employee at once
    D. discuss it as soon as possible with the employee

40. An office worker frequently complains to the custodian that her office is poorly illuminated.
    The BEST action for the custodian to follow is to
    A. ignore the complaints as those of an habitual crank
    B. inform the worker that illumination is a fixed item built into the building originally and evidently is the result of faulty planning by the architect
    C. request a licensed electrician to install additional ceiling lights
    D. investigate for faulty illumination features in the room, such as dirty lamp globes and incorrect lamp wattages

KEY (CORRECT ANSWERS)

1.	A	11.	D	21.	A	31.	D
2.	C	12.	D	22.	C	32.	B
3.	D	13.	A	23.	C	33.	C
4.	D	14.	D	24.	B	34.	D
5.	B	15.	B	25.	D	35.	C
6.	B	16.	A	26.	D	36.	B
7.	C	17.	B	27.	A	37.	C
8.	C	18.	A	28.	C	38.	D
9.	A	19.	B	29.	C	39.	D
10.	C	20.	B	30.	A	40.	D

TEST 2

DIRECTIONS: Each question or incomplete statement is followed by several suggested answers or completions. Select the one that BEST answers the question or completes the statement. *PRINT THE LETTER OF THE CORRECT ANSWER IN THE SPACE AT THE RIGHT.*

1. Of the following, the MOST important reason for the custodian to plan work schedules for men under his supervision is that
    A. emergency situations can easily be handled if they should arise
    B. it insures that essential operations will be adequately covered
    C. the men will be more satisfied if a routine is established
    D. the relationship between the supervisor and his subordinate will be clarified

    1.____

2. Sealers for open-grained wood floors should NOT contain linseed oil because
    A. the linseed oil would damage the wood fibers
    B. the linseed oil would deteriorate mop strands
    C. water wax would penetrate the linseed oil sealer and rot the wood
    D. linseed oil on wood take too long to dry satisfactorily before a floor finish could be applied

    2.____

3. When washing painted wall areas by hand, a man should be expected to wash each hour an area, in square feet, equal to
    A. 75-125   B. 150-300   C. 400-600   D. 750-1000

    3.____

4. Of the following, the one that is MOST desirable to use in dusting furniture is a
    A. feather duster   B. paper towel
    C. counter brush   D. soft cotton cloth

    4.____

5. The one of the following floor types on which oily sweeping compound may be used is
    A. vinyl tile   B. concrete   C. linoleum   D. terrazzo

    5.____

6. A steam heating system where the steam and condensate flow in the same pipe is called a _____ system.
    A. one pipe gravity return   B. sub-atmospheric
    C. vacuum return   D. zone control

    6.____

7. A test of a boiler by applying pressure equal to or greater than the maximum working pressure is called a ____ test.
    A. hydrostatic   B. barometric   C. hygroscopic   D. gyroscopic

    7.____

8. A stack switch, as used with an oil burner,
    A. shuts down the burner in case of non-ignition
    B. shuts down the burner in case of high stack temperatures
    C. controls the flow of secondary air
    D. operates the barometric damper

    8.____

9. The vertical pipes leading from the steam mains to the radiators are called
   A. drip lines
   B. risers
   C. radiant coils
   D. expansion joints

10. Fuel oil storage tanks are equipped with vents.
    The purpose of these vents is to
    A. make tank soundings
    B. check oil flash points
    C. fill the fuel tanks
    D. allow air to mix

11. A compound gauge in a boiler room
    A. measures steam and water pressure
    B. shows the quantity of boiler treatment compound on hand
    C. measures pressures above and below atmospheric pressure
    D. indicates the degree of compounding in a steam engine

12. Of the following, the CHIEF purpose of insulating steam lines is to
    A. prevent loss of heat
    B. protect people from being burned by them
    C. prevent leaks
    D. protect the pipes against corrosion

13. The MOST important function of thermostatic traps on radiators is to
    A. regulate the heat given off by the radiators
    B. remove water and air from the radiator
    C. assist the steam pressure in filling the radiator
    D. maintain a vacuum within the radiator

14. The designation *1/8-27N.P.T.* USUALLY indicates
    A. machine screw thread
    B. pipe thread
    C. spur gear size
    D. sprocket chain size

15. The size of a chisel is determined by its
    A. length   B. width   C. pitch   D. height

16. The cause of paint blisters is USUALLY
    A. moisture under the paint coat
    B. too thick a coat of paint
    C. too much oil in paint
    D. the plaster pores not sealed properly

17. A wood-framed picture is to be attached to a plaster and hollow tile wall.
    Of the following, the PROPER installation would include the use of
    A. wire cut nails
    B. miracle glue
    C. expansion shields and screws
    D. self-tapping screws

18. The PROPER tool or method to use for driving a finish nail to the depth necessary for puttying when installing wood trim is
    A. countersink
    B. another nail of the same diameter
    C. a nail set
    D. a center punch

    18.____

19. Faucet leakage in a large building is BEST controlled by periodic
    A. faucet replacement
    B. addition of a sealing compound to the water supply
    C. packing replacement
    D. faucet inspection and repair

    19.____

20. Escutcheons are USUALLY located
    A. on kitchen cabinet drawers
    B. on windows
    C. around pipes, to cover pipe sleeve openings
    D. around armored electric cable going into a gem box

    20.____

21. It is ADVISABLE to remove broken bulbs from light sockets with
    A. a wooden or hard rubber wedge
    B. pliers
    C. a hammer and chisel
    D. a fuse puller

    21.____

22. A room 20' x 25' in area with a ceiling height of 9'6" is to be painted. One gallon of paint will cover 400 square feet.
    The MINIMUM number of gallons necessary to give the four walls and the ceiling one coat of paint is
    A. 2   B. 3   C. 4   D. 5

    22.____

23. Of the following, the ones on which gaskets are MOST likely to be used are
    A threaded pipe plugs   B. cast iron pipe nipples
    C. flanged pipe fittings   D. threaded cast iron reducing tees

    23.____

24. If a 110 volt lamp were used on a 220 volt circuit, the
    A. fuse would burn out   B. lamp would burn out
    C. line would overheat   D. lamp would flicker

    24.____

25. The third prong on the plug of portable electric power tools of recent manufacture is for
    A. using the tool on a 3-phase power outlet
    B. eliminating interference in radio or television sets
    C. grounding the tool as a safety precaution
    D. using the tool on direct current circuits

    25.____

26. When changing brushes on a scrubbing machine, of the following, the FIRST step to take is to
    A. lock the switch in the *off* position
    B. be sure the power cable electric plug supplying the machine is disconnected from the wall outlet
    C. place the machine on top of the positioned brushes
    D. dip the brushes in water

27. In cleaning away branches that have been broken off as a result of a severe storm, one of your men comes in contact with a live electric line and falls unconscious.
    After having removed him from contact, the FIRST thing to be done is to
    A. send for an inhalator to revive him
    B. administer mouth-to-mouth resuscitation
    C. search for the switch to prevent any other such cases
    D. loosen his clothing and begin rubbing his forehead to restore circulation

28. Of the following, the MOST effective way to reduce waste in cleaning equipment and tools is by
    A. requiring a worn brush or broom to be returned before issuing a new one
    B. requiring the cleaners to use all cleaning tools for specific periods of time
    C. keeping careful records of how frequently cleaning equipment and tools are issued to cleaners
    D. making sure that cleaners use the tools properly

29. A window cleaner should carefully examine his safety belt
    A. once a week   B. before he puts it on each time
    C. once a month   D. once before he enters a building

30. One of your cleaners was injured as a result of slipping on an oily floor.
    This type of accident is MOST likely due to
    A. defective equipment
    B. the physical condition of the cleaner
    C. failure to use proper safety appliances
    D. poor housekeeping

31. One important use of accident reports is to provide information that may be used to reduce the possibility of similar accidents.
    The MOST valuable entry on the report for this purpose is the
    A. name of the victim   B. injury sustained by the victim
    C. cause of the accident   D. location of the accident

32. Fires in buildings are of such complexity that
    A. no plans or methods of attack can be formulated in advance
    B. no planned procedures can be relied on
    C. an appointed committee is necessary to direct fighting at the fire
    D. the problem must be considered in advance and methods of attack formulated

33. Of the following types of fires, a soda-acid fire extinguisher is NOT recommended for
    A. electric motor controls
    B. waste paper
    C. waste rags
    D. wood desks

34. A foam-type fire extinguisher extinguishes fires by
    A. cooling only
    B. drenching only
    C. smothering only
    D. cooling and smothering

35. If a keg of nails had on it the words *Net Weight 10 pounds*, it would mean that the
    A. keg weighed 10 pounds without the nails
    B. nails and the keg together weighed 10 pounds
    C. nails weighed 10 pounds without the keg
    D. weight of 10 pounds is approximate

36. In deciding which items should be stored together, the one of the following factors which is usually of LEAST importance is
    A. activity
    B. class
    C. cost
    D. size

37. Of the following, the MOST effective way to teach a subordinate how to store an item is to
    A. do it yourself while explaining
    B. explain the procedure verbally
    C. have him do it while you criticize
    D. let him look at photographs of the operation

38. If a cleaner is doing excellent work, then the PROPER action of the custodian is to
    A. give him preferential assignments as a reward
    B. tell the other cleaners what excellent work he is doing
    C. praise his work at the earlies opportunity
    D. do nothing since the man may become over-confident

39. A cleaner does very good work, but he has trouble getting to work on time. To get the man to come on time, you should
    A. bring him up on charges to stop the lateness once and for all
    B. have him report directly to you every time he is late
    C. talk over the problem with him to find its cause and possible solution
    D. threaten to transfer him if he cannot get to work on time

40. When the National flag is to be flown at half staff, it should ALWAYS be hoisted
    A. slowly to half staff
    B. slowly to the peak of staff and then lowered slowly to half staff
    C. briskly to the peak of staff and then lowered slowly to half staff
    D. briskly to the peak of staff and then lowered briskly to half staff

KEY (CORRECT ANSWERS)

1.	B	11.	C	21.	A	31.	C
2.	D	12.	A	22.	C	32.	D
3.	B	13.	B	23.	C	33.	A
4.	D	14.	B	24.	B	34.	D
5.	B	15.	B	25.	C	35.	C
6.	A	16.		26.	B	36.	C
7.	A	17.	C	27.	B	37.	A
8.	A	18.	C	28.	D	38.	C
9.	B	19.	C	29.	B	39.	C
10.	D	20.	D	30.	D	40.	C

EXAMINATION SECTION
TEST 1

DIRECTIONS: Each question or incomplete statement is followed by several suggested answers or completions. Select the one that BEST answers the question or completes the statement. *PRINT THE LETTER OF THE CORRECT ANSWER IN THE SPACE AT THE RIGHT.*

1. The flow of oil in an automatic rotary cup oil burner is regulated by a(n) 1.____

    A. thermostat
    B. metering valve
    C. pressure relief valve
    D. electric eye

2. The type of fuel which must be *pre-heated* before it can be burned efficiently is 2.____

    A. natural gas
    B. pea coal
    C. Number 2 oil
    D. Number 6 oil

3. A suction gauge in a fuel-oil transfer system is *usually* located 3.____

    A. *before* the strainer
    B. *after* the strainer and *before* the pump
    C. *after* the pump and *before* the pressure relief valve
    D. *after* the pressure relief valve

4. The FIRST item that should be checked before starting the fire in a steam boiler is the 4.____

    A. thermostat
    B. vacuum pump
    C. boiler water level
    D. steam pressure

5. Operation of a boiler that has been *sealed* by the department of buildings is 5.____

    A. prohibited
    B. permitted when the outside temperature is below 32° F
    C. permitted between the hours of 6:00 A.M. and 8:00 A.M. and 9:00 P.M. and 11:00 P.M.
    D. permitted only for the purposes of heating domestic water

6. Lowering the thermostat setting by 5 degrees during the heating season will result in a fuel saving of, *most nearly*, _____ percent. 6.____

    A. 2 B. 5 C. 20 D. 50

7. An electrically-driven rotary fuel oil pump must be protected from internal damage by the installation in the oil line of a 7.____

    A. discharge-side strainer
    B. check valve
    C. suction gauge
    D. pressure relief valve

8. The air pollution code states that no person shall cause or permit the emission of an air contaminant of a density which appears as dark or darker than Number _____ on the standard smoke chart. 8.____

    A. One
    B. Two
    C. Three
    D. Four

9. When a glass globe is put back over a newly-replaced light bulb in a ceiling light fixture, the holding screws on the globe should be tightened, then loosened one half turn. This is done MAINLY to prevent

    A. fires caused by electrical short circuits
    B. cracking of the globe due to heat expansion
    C. falling of the globe from the light fixture
    D. building up of harmful gases inside the globe

10. Standard 120-volt plug-type fuses are *generally* rated in

    A. farads   B. ohms   C. watts   D. amperes

11. Standard 120-volt electric light bulbs are *generally* rated in

    A. farads   B. ohms   C. watts   D. amperes

12. A cleaner informs you that his electrical vacuum cleaner is not working even though he tried the off-on switch several times and checked to see that the plug was still in the wall outlet.
    Of the following, the FIRST course of action you should take in this situation is to

    A. determine if the circuit-breaker has tripped out
    B. take apart the vacuum cleaner
    C. replace the electric cord on the vacuum cleaner
    D. replace the electrical outlet

13. The one of the following that is the MOST practical method for a building custodian to use in making a temporary repair in a straight portion of a water pipe which has a small leak is to

    A. attach a clamped patch over the leak
    B. weld or braze the pipe, depending on the material
    C. drill and tap the pipe, then insert a plug
    D. fill the hole with an epoxy sealer

14. The PRIMARY function of the packing which is generally found in the stuffing box of a centrifugal pump is to

    A. compensate for misalignment of the pump shaft
    B. prevent leakage of the fluid
    C. control the discharge rate of the pump
    D. provide support for the pump shaft

15. A pipe coupling is a plumbing fitting that is *most commonly* used to join

    A. two pieces of threaded pipe of the same diameter
    B. a large diameter tubing to a smaller diameter threaded pipe
    C. two pieces of threaded pipe of different diameters
    D. a large diameter threaded pipe to a smaller diameter tubing

16. Of the following, the MOST important reason for replacing a worn washer in a dripping faucet as soon as possible is to prevent

    A. overflow of the sink tap
    B. the mixture of hot and cold water in the sink
    C. damage to the faucet parts that can be the result of overtightening the stem
    D. air from entering the supply line

17. Window glass is secured mechanically in wood windows by

    A. glazing points   B. enamel paint
    C. screws   D. putty

18. In carpentry work, the *most commonly* used hand saw is the _____ saw.

    A. hack   B. rip   C. buck   D. cross-cut

19. The device which *usually* keeps a doorknob from rotating on the spindle is a

    A. cotter pin   B. tapered key
    C. set screw   D. stop screw

20. The *one* of the following types of nails that *usually* requires the use of a tool known as a nail set is the _____ nail.

    A. finishing   B. sheet rock   C. 6-penny   D. cut

21. The following tasks are frequently done when an office is cleaned:
    I. The floor is vacuumed.
    II. The ash trays and waste baskets are emptied.
    III. The desks and furniture are dusted.
    The ORDER in which these tasks should *generally* be done is:

    A. I, II, III   B. II, III, I   C. III, II, I   D. I, III, II

22. When wax is applied to a floor by the use of a twine mop with handle, the wax should be _____ with the mop.

    A. applied in thin coats
    B. applied in heavy coats
    C. poured on the floor, then spread
    D. dropped on the floor, then spread

23. The BEST way to clean dust from an accoustical-type ceiling is with a

    A. strong soap solution   B. wet sponge
    C. vacuum cleaner   D. stream of water

24. Of the following, the MOST important reason why a wet mop should NOT be wrung out by hand is that

    A. the strings of the mop will be damaged by hand-wringing
    B. sharp objects picked up by the mop may injure the hands
    C. the mop cannot be made dry enough by hand-wringing
    D. fine dirt will become embedded in the strings of the mop

25. When a painted wall is washed by hand, the wall should be washed from the

    A. *top down*, with a soaking *wet* sponge
    B. *bottom up*, with a soaking *wet* sponge
    C. *top down*, with a *damp* sponge
    D. *bottom up*, with a *damp* sponge

26. When a painted wall is brushed with a clean lamb's wool duster, the duster should be drawn _____ with a _____ pressure.

    A. *downward; light*
    B. *upward; light*
    C. *downward; firm*
    D. *upward; firm*

27. The *one* of the following terms which BEST describes the size of a floor brush is

    A. 72-cubic inch
    B. 32-ounce
    C. 24-inch
    D. 10-square foot

28. Terrazzo floors should be mopped periodically with a(n)

    A. acid solution
    B. neutral detergent in warm water
    C. mop treated with kerosene
    D. strong alkaline solution

29. The MAIN reason why the handle of a reversible floor brush should be shifted from one side of the brush block to the opposite side is to

    A. change the angle at which the brush sweeps the floor
    B. give equal wear to both sides of the brush
    C. permit the brush to sweep hard-to-reach areas
    D. make it easier to sweep backward

30. When a long corridor is swept with a floor brush, it is *good* practice to

    A. push the brush with moderately long strokes and flick it after each stroke
    B. press on the brush and push it the whole length of the corridor in one sweep
    C. pull the brush inward with short, brisk strokes
    D. sweep across rather than down the length of the corridor

KEY (CORRECT ANSWERS)

1.	B	16.	C
2.	D	17.	A
3.	B	18.	D
4.	C	19.	C
5.	A	20.	A
6.	C	21.	B
7.	D	22.	A
8.	B	23.	C
9.	B	24.	B
10.	D	25.	D
11.	C	26.	A
12.	A	27.	C
13.	A	28.	B
14.	B	29.	B
15.	A	30.	A

TEST 2

DIRECTIONS: Each question or incomplete statement is followed by several suggested answers or completions. Select the one that BEST answers the question or completes the statement. *PRINT THE LETTER OF THE CORRECT ANSWER IN THE SPACE AT THE RIGHT.*

1. Of the following office cleaning jobs performed during the year, the *one* which should be done MOST frequently is

    A. cleaning the fluorescent lights
    B. dusting the Venetian blinds
    C. cleaning the bookcase glass
    D. carpet-sweeping the rug

2. The BEST polishing agent to use on wood furniture is

    A. pumice
    B. paste wax
    C. water emulsion wax
    D. neat's-foot oil

3. Lemon oil polish is used BEST to polish

    A. exterior bronze
    B. marble walls
    C. leather seats
    D. lacquered metal

4. Cleaning with trisodium phosphate is *most likely* to damage

    A. toilet bowls
    B. drain pipes
    C. polished marble floors
    D. rubber tile floors

5. Of the following cleaning agents, the one which should NOT be used to remove stains from urinals is

    A. caustic lye
    B. detergent
    C. oxalic acid
    D. muriatic acid

6. The one of the following cleaners which *generally* contains an abrasive is

    A. caustic lye
    B. trisodium phosphate
    C. scouring powder
    D. ammonia

7. The instructions on a box of cleaning powder say: *Mix one pound of cleaning powder in four gallons of water.* According to these instructions, how many ounces of cleaning powder should be mixed in one gallon of water?

    A. 4   B. 8   C. 12   D. 16

8. In accordance with recommended practice, a dust mop, when not being used, should be stored

    A. *hanging,* handle end down
    B. *hanging,* handle end up
    C. *standing* on the floor, handle end down
    D. *standing* on the floor, handle end up

9. The two types of floors found in public buildings are classified as *hard floors* and *soft floors*.
An example of a *hard floor* is one made of

   A. linoleum
   B. cork
   C. ceramic tile
   D. asphalt tile

10. A squeegee is a tool that is MAINLY used to clean

    A. painted walls
    B. radiator covers
    C. window glass
    D. ceramic tile floors

11. The BEST way for a building custodian to determine whether a cleaner is doing his work well is by

    A. observing the cleaner at work for several hours
    B. asking the cleaner questions about the work
    C. asking other cleaners to rate his work
    D. inspecting the cleanliness of the spaces assigned to the cleaner

12. The PRIMARY purpose of using a disinfectant material is to

    A. kill germs
    B. destroy odors
    C. remove stains
    D. kill insects

13. Windows should be washed by using a solution of warm water mixed with

    A. chlorine bleach
    B. kerosene
    C. ammonia
    D. soft soap

14. Of the following, the MOST effective way to reduce waste of cleaning tools is to

    A. keep careful records of how often tools are issued
    B. require that the old tool be returned before issuing a new one
    C. require that all tools be used for a fixed number of hours before replacing them
    D. train the cleaners to use the tools properly

15. The number of square feet of unobstructed corridor floor space that a cleaner should sweep in an hour is, *most nearly,*

    A. 1200   B. 2400   C. 4000   D. 6000

16. Sweeping compound is used on concrete floors MAINLY to

    A. polish the floor
    B. keep the dust down
    C. soften the encrusted dirt
    D. provide a non-slip surface

17. The BEST attachment to use on an electric scrubbing machine when stripping waxed resilient flooring is a

    A. nylon disk
    B. soft brush
    C. steel wool pad
    D. pumice wheel

18. A counter brush is BEST suited to cleaning

    A. water cooler drains
    B. radiators
    C. light fixtures
    D. lavatory fixtures

19. Improper use of a carbon-dioxide type portable fire extinguisher may cause injury to the operator because

    A. handling the nozzle during discharge can cause frostbite to the skin
    B. carbon dioxide is highly poisonous if breathed into the lungs
    C. use of carbon dioxide on an oil fire can cause a chemical explosion
    D. the powdery residue left by the discharge is highly caustic to the skin

20. When using a portable single ladder with ten rungs, the GREATEST number of rungs that a cleaner should climb up is

    A. 7   B. 8   C. 9   D. 10

21. Of the following types of portable fire extinguishers, the one which should be used to control a fire in or around live electrical equipment is the _____ type.

    A. foam
    B. soda-acid
    C. carbon-dioxide
    D. gas-cartridge water

22. The MOST frequent cause of accidental injuries to workers on the job is

    A. unsafe working practices of employees
    B. poor design of buildings and working areas
    C. lack of warning signs in hazardous working areas
    D. lack of adequate safety guards on equipment and machinery

23. Of the following, the MOST important purpose of preparing an accident report on an injury to a cleaner is to help

    A. collect statistics on different types of accidents
    B. calm the feelings of the injured cleaner
    C. prevent similar accidents in the future
    D. prove that the cleaner was at fault

24. The one of the following types of locks that is used on emergency exit doors is the _____ bolt.

    A. panic   B. dead   C. cinch   D. toggle

25. The one of the following types of locks that *usually* contains both a live bolt and a dead bolt is a _____ lock.

    A. mortise
    B. double-hung window
    C. loose pin butt
    D. window frame

KEY (CORRECT ANSWERS)

1.	D	11.	D
2.	B	12.	A
3.	A	13.	C
4.	C	14.	D
5.	D	15.	D
6.	C	16.	B
7.	A	17.	A
8.	B	18.	B
9.	C	19.	A
10.	C	20.	B

21. C
22. A
23. C
24. A
25. A

EXAMINATION SECTION
TEST 1

DIRECTIONS: Each question or incomplete statement is followed by several suggested answers or completions. Select the one that BEST answers the question or completes the statement. *PRINT THE LETTER OF THE CORRECT ANSWER IN THE SPACE AT THE RIGHT.*

1. Oil soaked waste and rags *should be*

    A. deposited in a self-closing metal can
    B. piled in the open
    C. stored in the supply closet
    D. rolled up and be available for the next job

2. Inspection for safety should be included as part of the custodian-engineer's _____ inspection.

    A. daily   B. weekly
    C. monthly   D. quarterly

3. Of the following classifications, the one which pertains to fires in electrical equipment is Class _____.

    A. A   B. B   C. C   D. D

4. The type of portable fire extinguisher which is *particularly* suited for extinguishing flammable liquid fires is the _____ type.

    A. soda-acid   B. foam
    C. pump tank   D. loaded stream

5. Of the following liquids, the one which has the LOWEST flash point is

    A. kerosene   B. gasoline
    C. benzene   D. carbon tetrachloride

6. When giving first aid to an injured person, which *one* of the following should you NOT do?

    A. Administer medication internally
    B. Send for a physician
    C. Control bleeding
    D. Treat for shock

7. In reference to fire fighting, fires are of such complexity that

    A. no plans or methods of attack can be formulated in advance
    B. the problem must be considered in advance and methods of attack formulated
    C. an appointed committee is necessary to direct fighting at the fire
    D. no planned procedures can be relied on

8. The heat of a soldering copper should be tested

    A. with solder
    B. by holding it near kraft paper

C. by holding it near your hand
D. with water

9. Safety on the job is BEST assured by

   A. keeping alert
   B. following every rule
   C. working very slowly
   D. never working alone

10. One important use of accident reports is to provide information that may be used to reduce the possibility of similar accidents.
    The MOST valuable entry on the report for this purpose is the

    A. time lost due to accident
    B. date of the occurrence
    C. injury sustained by victim
    D. cause of the accident

11. Suppose that you are the custodian-engineer and an employee works for you at the rate of $8.70 per hour with time and one-half paid for time worked after 40 hours in one week. His gross pay for working 53 hours in one week is, *most nearly,*

    A. $461.10   B. $482.10   C. $487.65   D. $517.65

12. Suppose that you are the custodian-engineer and one of your employees has gotten gross earnings of $437.10 for the week, all of which is subject to Social Security deductions at the rate of 7.05%.
    The amount which should be deducted from the employee's gross earnings for the week is, *most nearly,*

    A. $21.70   B. $28.40   C. $29.32   D. $30.82

13. The MINIMUM number of gate valves usually required in a by-pass around a steam trap is

    A. 1   B. 2   C. 3   D. 4

14. A 2-inch standard steel pipe, as compared with a 2-inch extra-heavy steel pipe, has the *same*

    A. wall thickness
    B. inside diameter
    C. outside diameter
    D. weight per linear foot

15. A short piece of pipe with a standard male pipe thread on one end and a locknut thread on the other end is *usually* called a(n)

    A. close nipple
    B. tank nipple
    C. coupling
    D. union

16. Dies are used by plumbers to

    A. ream out the inside of pipes
    B. thread pipes
    C. bevel the ends of pipes
    D. make-up solder joints

17. Of the following types of pipe, the one which is MOST brittle is   17._____

    A. brass   B. copper
    C. cast iron   D. wrought iron

18. The PRIMARY function of a trap in a drainage system is to   18._____

    A. prevent gases from flowing into the building
    B. produce an efficient flushing action
    C. prevent articles accidentally dropped into the drainage system from entering the sewer
    D. prevent the water backing up

19. If a plumbing fixture is allowed to stand unused for a long time, its trap is apt to lose its seal by   19._____

    A. evaporation   B. capillary action
    C. siphonage   D. condensation

20. The pipe fitting used to connect a 14" pipe directly to a 1" pipe in a straight line is called a(n)   20._____

    A. union   B. nipple   C. elbow   D. reducer

21. The BEST procedure to follow when replacing a blown fuse is to   21._____

    A. immediately replace it with the same size fuse
    B. immediately replace it with a larger size fuse
    C. immediately replace it with a smaller size fuse
    D. correct the cause of the fuse failure and replace it with the correct size

22. The amperage rating of the fuse to be used in an electrical circuit is determined by the   22._____

    A. size of the connected load
    B. size of the wire in the circuit
    C. voltage of the circuit
    D. ambient temperature

23. In a 208-volt, 3-phase, 4-wire circuit, the voltage, in volts, from any line to the grounded neutral is, *approximately,*   23._____

    A. 208   B. 150   C. 120   D. zero

24. The device *commonly* used to change an A.C. voltage to a D.C. voltage is called a   24._____

    A. transformer   B. rectifier
    C. relay   D. capacitor or condenser

25. Where conduit enters a knock-out in an outlet box, it should be provided with a   25._____

    A. bushing on the inside and outside with a locknut
    B. locknut on the inside and bushing on the outside
    C. union on the outside and a nipple on the inside
    D. nipple on the outside and a union on the inside

KEY (CORRECT ANSWERS)

1.	A	11.	D
2.	A	12.	D
3.	C	13.	C
4.	B	14.	C
5.	B	15.	B
6.	A	16.	B
7.	B	17.	C
8.	A	18.	A
9.	A	19.	A
10.	D	20.	D

21. D
22. B
23. C
24. B
25. A

TEST 2

DIRECTIONS: Each question or incomplete statement is followed by several suggested answers or completions. Select the one that BEST answers the question or completes the Statement. *PRINT THE LETTER OF THE CORRECT ANSWER IN THE SPACE AT THE RIGHT.*

1. The electric circuit to a ten kilowatt electric hot water heater which is automatically controlled by an aquastat will *also* require a

    A. transistor
    B. choke coil
    C. magnetic contactor
    D. limit switch

    1.____

2. An electric power consumption meter usually indicates the power used in

    A. watts
    B. volt-hours
    C. amperes
    D. kilowatt-hours

    2.____

3. Of the following sizes of copper wire, the one which can *safely* carry the GREATEST amount of amperes is

    A. 14 ga. stranded
    B. 12 ga. stranded
    C. 12 ga. solid
    D. 10 ga. solid

    3.____

4. A flexible coupling is PRIMARILY used to

    A. allow for imperfect alignment of two joining shafts
    B. allow for slight differences in shaft diameters
    C. insure perfect alignment of the joining shafts
    D. reduce fast starting of the machinery

    4.____

5. The one of the following statements concerning lubricating oil which is CORRECT is:

    A. SAE 10 is heavier and more viscous than SAE 30.
    B. Diluting lubricating oil with gasoline increases its viscosity
    C. Oil reduces friction between moving parts
    D. In hot weather, thin oil is preferable to heavy oil

    5.____

6. The MAIN purpose of periodic inspections and tests made on mechanical equipment is to

    A. make the operating men familiar with the equipment
    B. keep the maintenance men busy during otherwise slack periods
    C. discover minor faults before they develop into serious breakdowns
    D. encourage the men to take better care of the equipment

    6.____

7. The one of the following bearing types which is NOT classified as a roller bearing is

    A. radial   B. angular   C. thrust   D. babbitt

    7.____

8. In a wire rope, when a number of wires are laid left-handed into a strand and the strand laid right-handed around a hemp rope center, the wire rope is *commonly* known as a

    A. right-lay, Lang-lay rope
    B. left-lay, Lang-lay rope
    C. left-lay, regular-lay rope
    D. right-lay, regular-lay rope

    8.____

37

9. The chemical which is NOT used for disinfecting swimming pools is 9.___

   A. ammonia
   B. calcium hypochloride
   C. chlorine
   D. liquified chlorine

10. The one of the following V-belt sections which has the HIGHEST horsepower-belt rating is _____ section 10.___

    A. A
    B. B
    C. C
    D. D

11. An air compressor which is driven by an electric motor is *usually* started and stopped automatically by a(n) 11.___

    A. unloader
    B. pressure regulator valve
    C. float switch
    D. pressure switch

12. The volume in cubic feet of a cylindrical tank, 6 ft. in diameter by 35 ft. long, is, *most nearly*, 12.___

    A. 210
    B. 990
    C. 1,260
    D. 3,960

13. If the directions given by your superior are NOT clear, the BEST thing for you to do is to 13.___

    A. ask to have the directions repeated and clarified
    B. proceed to do the work taking a chance on doing the right thing
    C. do nothing until some later time when you can find out exactly what is wanted
    D. ask one of the other men in your crew what he would do under the circumstances

14. Of the following procedures concerning grievances of subordinate personnel, the custodian-engineer should maintain an attitude of 14.___

    A. paying little attention to little grievances
    B. being very alert to grievances and make adjustments in existing conditions to appease all personnel
    C. knowing the most frequent causes of grievances and strive to prevent them from arising
    D. maintain rigid discipline of a nature that smoothes out all grievances

15. Of the following, the BEST course of action to take to settle a dispute or conflict between two employees is to 15.___

    A. insist that the two employees settle the case between themselves
    B. call in each one separately and, after hearing their cases presented, decide the issue
    C. bring both in for a conference at the same time and make the decision in their presence
    D. have both present their points of view and arguments in written memoranda and, on this basis, make your decision

16. If, as a custodian-engineer, you discover an error in your report submitted to the main office, you should 16.___

    A. do nothing, since it is possible that one error will have little effect on the total report
    B. wait until the error is discovered in the main office and then offer to work overtime to correct it
    C. go directly to the supervisor in the main office after working hours and ask him unofficially to correct the error
    D. notify the main office immediately so that the error can be corrected, if necessary

17. There are a considerable number of forms and reports to be submitted on schedule by   17._____
    the custodian-engineer. The *advisable* method of accomplishing this duty is to

    A. fill out the reports at off times during the days when you have free time
    B. schedule a definite period to the work week for completing these forms and reports
    C. assign your foremen or cleaner to handle all these forms for you and to have them available on time
    D. classify or group the forms and reports and fill out only one of each group and refer the other forms or reports to the ones completed

18. A custodian-engineer can BEST evaluate the quality of work performed by custodial personnel by   18._____

    A. periodic inspection of the building's cleanliness
    B. studying the time records or personnel
    C. reviewing the building cleaning expenditures
    D. analyzing complaints of building occupants

19. Assume that you are the custodian-engineer and one of your employees wants to talk   19._____
    with you about a grievance. Of the following actions, the LEAST desirable action for you to take is to

    A. listen sympathetically
    B. conduct the discussion openly in the presence of the workforce
    C. try to get his point of view
    D. endeavor to obtain all the facts

20. Of the following factors, the one which is LEAST important in evaluating an employee   20._____
    and his work is his

    A. dependability   B. quantity of work
    C. quality of work   D. education and training

21. Supervision of a group of people engaged in building cleaning operations should NOT   21._____
    include supervision of

    A. time spent in cleaning operations
    B. utilization of official rest and lunch periods
    C. cleaning methods
    D. materials used for various cleaning jobs

22. Of the following methods, the BEST one to utilize in assigning custodial personnel to   22._____
    clean a multi-floor public building, is to

    A. allow the cleaners to pick their rooms or area assignment out of a hat
    B. have the supervisor make specific room or area assignments to each cleaner separately
    C. rotate room and area assignments daily according to a chart posted on the bulletin board
    D. let a different member of the group make the room or area assignments each week

23. Assume that you are the custodian-engineer and that you have discovered a bottle of liquor in one of your employees' locker.
The BEST course of action to take is to

     A. fire him immediately
     B. explain to him that liquor should not be brought into a school building and that a repetition may result in disciplinary action
     C. suspend him until the end of the week and take him back only on a probational basis
     D. assemble the staff and tell them they are all equally guilty for not having reported the matter to you

24. Of the following items, the one which is the LEAST important in the preparation of a report is that the report

     A. is brief, but to the point
     B. uses the prescribed form if there is one
     C. contains extra copies
     D. is accurate

25. In order to have building employees willing to follow standardized cleaning and maintenance procedures, the supervisor must *be prepared to*

     A. work alongside the employees
     B. demonstrate the reasonableness of the procedures
     C. offer incentive pay for their utilization
     D. allow the employees the free use of the time saved by their adoption

KEY (CORRECT ANSWERS)

1.	C	11.	D
2.	D	12.	B
3.	D	13.	A
4.	A	14.	C
5.	C	15.	C
6.	C	16.	D
7.	D	17.	B
8.	D	18.	A
9.	A	19.	B
10.	D	20.	D

21. B
22. B
23. B
24. C
25. B

EXAMINATION SECTION
TEST 1

DIRECTIONS: Each question or incomplete statement is followed by several suggested answers or completions. Select the one that BEST answers the question or completes the statement. *PRINT THE LETTER OF THE CORRECT ANSWER IN THE SPACE AT THE RIGHT.*

1. A chemical frequently used to melt ice on outdoor pavements is 1.____

   A. ammonia
   B. soda
   C. carbon tetrachloride
   D. calcium chloride

2. A herbicide is a chemical PRIMARILY used as a(n) 2.____

   A. disinfectant
   B. fertilizer
   C. insect killer
   D. weed killer

3. Established plants that continue to blossom year after year without reseeding are GENERALLY known as 3.____

   A. annuals
   B. parasites
   C. perennials
   D. symbiotics

4. A ferrous sulfate solution is sometimes used to treat shrubs or trees that have a deficiency of 4.____

   A. boron   B. copper   C. iron   D. zinc

5. A tree is described as *deciduous*. This means that it 5.____

   A. bears nuts instead of fruit
   B. has been pruned recently
   C. usually grows in swampy ground
   D. loses its leaves in fall

6. The landscape drawings for a school indicate the planting of *Acer platanoides* at a certain location on the grounds. Acer platanoides is a type of 6.____

   A. privet hedge
   B. rose bush
   C. maple tree
   D. tulip bed

7. After a snowfall has stopped, the law requires that all snow be removed from sidewalks within _____ hour(s). 7.____

   A. 4   B. 3   C. 2   D. 1

8. When roofing material is specified as 5 *ply, 70 lbs.*, it means that, as laid, the total of 5 plies weighs 70 lbs. per 100 8.____

   A. square feet
   B. yards length
   C. square inches
   D. feet length

43

9. Little white insects that look like small shrimps and feed on the roots of grass are called

   A. grubs
   B. ticks
   C. praying mantes
   D. crabs

10. A term used to indicate a lawn chemical weed killer is

    A. germicide
    B. emulsified
    C. herbicide
    D. vitrified

11. Before starting any lawn mowing, the distance between the blade and a flat surface should be measured with a ruler. This distance should be such that the cut of the grass above the ground is _____ inch(es).

    A. 1
    B. 1½
    C. 2
    D. 3

12. *Neat* cement is a mixture of cement

    A. putty and water
    B. and water
    C. lime and water
    D. salt and water

13. In a concrete mix of 1:2:4, the 2 refers to the amount of

    A. sand
    B. cement
    C. stone
    D. water

14. If it is not possible to plant new shrubs immediately upon delivery in the spring, they should be stored in a(n)

    A. sheltered outdoor area
    B. unsheltered outdoor area
    C. boiler room
    D. warm place indoors

15. To remove chalk marks on sidewalks and cemented playground areas, the MOST acceptable cleaning method is

    A. using a brush with warm water
    B. using a brush with warm water containing some kerosene
    C. hosing down such areas with water
    D. using a brush with a solution of muriatic acid in water

16. The *10* in a 10-6-4 mixture stands for the amount of

    A. phoric acid
    B. oxygen
    C. potash
    D. nitrogen

17. Turning over of a lawn is BEST performed during the

    A. spring
    B. summer
    C. fall
    D. winter

18. When watering lawns, an open top can should be placed near the sprinkler and watering should be stopped when the can is filled to a depth of _____ inch(es).

    A. ½
    B. 1
    C. 1½
    D. 2

19. Powered lawnmowers should be filled with gas ONLY

    A. in the boiler room
    B. in the outside storeroom
    C. outdoors
    D. when running

Questions 20-22.

DIRECTIONS: Questions 20 through 22 are to be answered on the basis of the following paragraph.

Whether a main lobby or upper corridor requires scrubbing or mopping and whether it should be done nightly or less frequently depends on the nature of the floor surface and the amount of traffic. In a building with heavy traffic, it may be desirable every night to scrub the main lobby and to mop the upper floors. In such cases, it may also be found desirable to scrub the upper floors once a week. If traffic is light, it may only be necessary to mop the main lobby every other night and to mop the upper floor corridors once a week. If there is any traffic or usage at all, it will be necessary to at least sweep the corridors nightly.

20. According to the above paragraph, in a building with light traffic, the upper floors and corridors should be

    A. swept every other night
    B. mopped every night
    C. swept nightly
    D. mopped every other night

21. The number of times a floor is cleaned depends

    A. mainly on the type of floor surface
    B. mainly on the type of traffic
    C. only on the amount of traffic
    D. on both the floor surface and the amount of traffic

22. It may be desirable to have a heavily used main lobby swept

    A. daily and scrubbed weekly
    B. daily and mopped weekly
    C. and mopped weekly
    D. and scrubbed daily

23. Interior fire alarm systems are tested

    A. daily   B. weekly
    C. every Saturday   D. never

24. An electrical meter is read from

    A. left to right   B. right to left
    C. closest high number   D. closest low number

25. A light bulb socket has the threaded shell connected to _____ wire(s).

    A. neither hot nor ground   B. ground
    C. hot   D. hot and ground

KEY (CORRECT ANSWERS)

1.	D	11.	C
2.	D	12.	B
3.	C	13.	A
4.	C	14.	A
5.	D	15.	A
6.	C	16.	D
7.	A	17.	C
8.	A	18.	B
9.	A	19.	C
10.	C	20.	C |''

21. D
22. D
23. A
24. A
25. B

TEST 2

DIRECTIONS: Each question or incomplete statement is followed by several suggested answers or completions. Select the one that BEST answers the question or completes the statement. *PRINT THE LETTER OF THE CORRECT ANSWER IN THE SPACE AT THE RIGHT.*

1. The purpose of an air valve in a heating system is to   1.____

    A. prevent pressure build-up in a room
    B. relieve air from radiators
    C. allow excess steam to escape from boiler
    D. control room temperature

2. A scale pocket is MOST often found on the   2.____

    A. bottom of steam riser   B. hot air exhaust grills
    C. hot water radiator   D. inside of the steam radiator

3. Ventilation of rooms without windows is accomplished by   3.____

    A. opening and closing room doors
    B. heating and cooling of room by radiators
    C. mechanical circulation and exhausting through ducts
    D. use of air deodorizers

4. When a radiator in a one-pipe gravity system is air-bound, the MOST likely cause is   4.____

    A. a defective air valve
    B. air entering through leaking valve
    C. insufficient steam pressure
    D. a defective gate valve

5. When a radiator in a two-pipe gravity system is air-bound, the MOST likely cause is   5.____

    A. a defective air valve
    B. air entering through leaking valve
    C. insufficient steam pressure
    D. a defective gate valve

6. A vacuum heating system does NOT have   6.____

    A. traps   B. pneumatic valves
    C. risers   D. air valves

7. In a one-pipe gravity return system,   7.____

    A. piping is large   B. piping is small
    C. valves can be throttled D. vacuum pumps are used

8. One of the advantages of a vacuum system of heating is   8.____

    A. high maintenance costs
    B. use of electricity
    C. low pressure steam circulation
    D. cannot install radiation below the water line

9. A plenum chamber is where

   A. fresh air is filtered
   B. fresh air is heated
   C. returns are heated
   D. steam is reheated

10. Air picks up heat and moisture when compressed. Because of this, compressed air storage tanks should be drained

    A. daily
    B. when gauge glass is full
    C. monthly
    D. weekly

11. The _____ safety devices will shut down an oil burner in the event of flame failure.

    A. fireye
    B. flame rod
    C. stack switch
    D. all of the above

12. Steam is used to heat fuel oil.
    After it has condensed to water, it is

    A. blown down to waste
    B. returned to boiler
    C. used for heating coils
    D. recirculated

13. Relief valves throughout oil flow systems guard the system against excess

    A. temperature
    B. vacuum
    C. pressure
    D. all of the above

14. A transformer is used to raise line voltage for an ignition system.
    This type of voltage increase can be called a(n)

    A. rheostat
    B. amplifying circuit
    C. compensating motor
    D. electrode

15. A device which basically causes hi and low fire conditions in an oil burner is called a

    A. modutrol motor
    B. hi-limit pressuretrol
    C. primary air fan casing
    D. metering valve

16. A device that mixes the proper amount of oil, primary air, and secondary air for combustion is called a

    A. modutrol motor
    B. hi-limit pressuretrol
    C. primary air fan casing
    D. metering valve

17. A device which stops an oil burner in the event of pressuretrol failure is called a

    A. modutrol motor
    B. hi-limit pressuretrol
    C. primary air fan casing
    D. metering valve

18. If the heart of an oil flow system and oil burner operation is the fuel oil transfer pump, the *brain* of this system could be called the

    A. stack switch
    B. aquastat
    C. ringelmann
    D. programmer

19. The spinning cup of the oil burner should be cleaned daily. If oil deposits have hardened on the spinning cup, you should clean it with

    A. a smooth wood or plastic stick
    B. a file
    C. sandpaper
    D. 00 steel wool

20. The BEST method of connecting two No. 14 electrical fixture wires together is with 20.____

    A. solder
    B. screw and nut
    C. tape
    D. twist wires together

21. A safety device used instead of a fuse to protect electrical equipment against overload is a 21.____

    A. rheostat
    B. circuit breaker
    C. relay
    D. toggle switch

22. Piping used to carry exposed electrical wiring is called 22.____

    A. conductors
    B. sleeves
    C. conduit
    D. leaders

23. Knife switches may be made to work more easily by using 23.____

    A. vaseline   B. graphite   C. soapstone   D. grease

24. Hidden electrical wiring is carried in 24.____

    A. conduit   B. raceway   C. conductors   D. BX cable

25. A T-40 could be BEST described as a(n) 25.____

    A. fuse
    B. incandescent lamp
    C. fluorescent bulb
    D. circuit breaker

KEY (CORRECT ANSWERS)

1. B		11. D	
2. A		12. A	
3. C		13. C	
4. A		14. B	
5. A		15. D	
6. D		16. A	
7. A		17. B	
8. C		18. D	
9. B		19. A	
10. D		20. A	

21. B
22. C
23. C
24. D
25. B

EXAMINATION SECTION
TEST 1

DIRECTIONS: Each question or incomplete statement is followed by several suggested answers or completions. Select the one that BEST answers the question or completes the statement. *PRINT THE LETTER OF THE CORRECT ANSWER IN THE SPACE AT THE RIGHT.*

1. The safety device on an elevator door is called the　　　　　　　　　　　1.____
    A. governor　　B. gate-switch　　C. interlock　　D. safety fuse

2. Which of the following is the PROPER method of cleaning a room?　　2.____
    A. Dust, empty wastebasket, sweep
    B. Empty wastebasket, dust, sweep
    C. Empty wastebasket, sweep, dust
    D. Sweep, dust, empty wastebasket

3. How would you determine when a waxed floor should be stripped?　　3.____
   When
    A. someone slipped on the floor
    B. wax builds up
    C. scuffs are not removed by buffing
    D. someone complains

4. To remove modeling plaster from the floor, you should use　　　　　　4.____
    A. a sharp chisel　　　　　　　B. a putty knife
    C. a floor-scrubbing machine　　D. sulphuric acid

5. Which of the following floors would you NOT seal?　　　　　　　　　　5.____
    A. Terrazzo　　B. Cork　　C. Asphalt　　D. Tile

6. A mixing valve for domestic water blends　　　　　　　　　　　　　　6.____
    A. cold water with hot boiler water
    B. hot and cold water
    C. cold water and hot water from coil submerged in boiler water
    D. hot and cold water from cooling coil

7. For sweeping under the radiators, the BEST tool to use is a　　　　　7.____
    A. dry mop　　　　　　B. feather duster
    C. counter brush　　　D. floor broom

8. A wet return line is　　　　　　　　　　　　　　　　　　　　　　　　8.____
    A. one containing air and water　　B. above boiler water level
    C. below boiler water level　　　　D. a condenser oil

9. A dry return line is
   A. one containing air only
   B. above boiler water level
   C. one containing air and water
   D. a line with a bleeder valve

10. The purpose of a fusetron is to
    A. provide motor starting current
    B. keep motor at rated speed
    C. protect from overload
    D. maintain constant motor speed

11. If combination faucet is in off position and water leaks from swivel, you should
    A. replace faucet washers
    B. repack swivel gland
    C. replace both washers and tighten swivel gland
    D. replace the faucet

12. The MAIN purpose of peat moss use is to
    A. improve soil condition
    B. fertilize soil
    C. help to keep soil moist
    D. retard the growth of weeds

13. Which of the following valves does NOT have a wheel and stem?
    A. Globe
    B. Gate
    C. Check
    D. Plug cock

14. If a radiator is air-bound, the MOST likely cause is
    A. no condensate return
    B. defective steam valve
    C. defective air valve
    D. too much air carried in steam

15. The MAIN purpose of keeping accident reports on file is to
    A. have a record to show a lawyer
    B. contain cause of accident
    C. inform principal of how it happened
    D. provide full information for official use

16. To repair a continually flushing flushometer, you should
    A. cut down on supply valve
    B. shut off water
    C. clean out flushometer
    D. replace defective parts

17. When a repair is required, the LEAST likely thing to be done is:
    A. Determine if your staff can handle it
    B. Find out just what has to be done
    C. Ask for assistance from repair shops
    D. Decide which tools are needed to do the job

18. At which of the following locations should you find a remote control switch?
    A. In principal's office
    B. In engineer's office
    C. At boiler room entrance
    D. At entrance to building

19. Sprinkler systems are more often found in the following location:
    A. Boiler room
    B. Gym
    C. Storage rooms
    D. Science rooms

20. If a gas range flame is all whitish yellow, what does it indicate?
    A. Insufficient gas pressure
    B. Insufficient air
    C. Not enough gas
    D. Too much air

20.____

21. If glass on water column breaks when boiler is operating, you should
    A. bank fire
    B. shut off burner
    C. use tri-cocks
    D. close main steam valve

21.____

22. The BEST reason for setting a time limit on the job is
    A. time available
    B. if completion is urgent
    C. if maximum output is affected this way
    D. the men are more likely to complete the job on time

22.____

23. The safety device on a gas line is called
    A. gas cock
    B. automatic pilot
    C. solenoid valve
    D. safety shut-off valve

23.____

24. The MOST efficient boiler fuel operation is
    A. low CO_2 high CO, low stack gas temperature
    B. high CO_2 low CO, low stack gas temperature
    C. high firebox temperature, high CO_2 high stack temperature
    D. high CO_2 low CO, high stack gas temperature

24.____

25. The central vacuum cleaning system should be cleaned
    A. weekly
    B. twice weekly
    C. daily
    D. when necessary

25.____

26. If you had too much oil, what would you do for good combustion?
    A. Increase secondary air
    B. Increase primary air
    C. Increase both
    D. Lower oil pressure

26.____

27. The purpose of blowing down the water column is to
    A. make sure there is enough water
    B. keep the gauge glass clean
    C. determine the true water level
    D. make sure you have steam in boiler

27.____

28. Water hammer in water lines is caused by
    A. velocity of air and water
    B. defective faucet
    C. defective washers
    D. quick opening and closing of faucets

28.____

29. The CHIEF reason for a plumbing system trap is to
    A. equalize waste
    B. provide good drainage
    C. provide water seal
    D. none of the above

29.____

30. A vapor barrier is used for
    A. insulating electrically
    B. protecting against low temperature
    C. a moisture barrier
    D. exterior condensation on cold water pipes

31. The material recommended for removing blood or fruit stains from concrete is
    A. soft soap   B. neatsfoot oil   C. oxalic acid   D. ammonia

32. For what purpose are panic bars used? To
    A. make sure door is locked   B. provide easy exit
    C. meet fire department regulations D. keep door open

33. To detect a leak in the gas line, which of the following would you do?
    A. Call gas company   B. Use a soapy solution
    C. Use a lighted match   D. Smell the area

34. To preserve freshly laid concrete, you would
    A. cover it   B. keep it moist
    C. keep it at a temperature of 60°F C. keep it at a temperature over 60°F

35. Gas is measured in
    A. thousands cubic feet   B. hundreds cubic feet
    C. ten thousands cubic feet volume   D. 100,000 cubic feet volume

36. The FIRST thing a window cleaner should do is
    A. test window bolts   B. see that cleaning tools are good
    C. check window belt   D. not lean too heavily on glass

37. Couplings on gas supply line serve the same purpose as
    A. electrical conduit   B. machine threads
    C. right and left hand   D. water unions

38. Before a custodian leaves the building, he would be LEAST likely to
    A. lower the flag   B. remove hazards
    C. tidy the stock room   D. check all entry doors

39. Which of the following would you NOT use to paint chain-link fences?
    A. Brush   B. Sprayer
    C. Roller   D. None of the above

40. Which of the following steps should be taken in closing a low pressure boiler at the end of heating season in preparation for lay-up?
    A. Empty water, close valves, drop fire
    B. Dump fire, close valves, let boiler cool, empty water
    C. Dump fire, let boiler cool, empty water, close valves
    D. None of the above

KEY (CORRECT ANSWERS)

1.	C	11.	A	21.	C	31.	D
2.	C	12.	C	22.	D	32.	B
3.	B	13.	C	23.	C	33.	B
4.	B	14.	C	24.	B	34.	B
5.	C	15.	D	25.	B	35.	A
6.	B	16.	D	26.	B	36.	C
7.	C	17.	C	27.	C	37.	C
8.	C	18.	C	28.	A	38.	C
9.	B	19.	C	29.	C	39.	B
10.	C	20.	D	30.	C	40.	B

TEST 2

DIRECTIONS: Each question or incomplete statement is followed by several suggested answers or completions. Select the one that BEST answers the question or completes the statement. *PRINT THE LETTER OF THE CORRECT ANSWER IN THE SPACE AT THE RIGHT.*

1. The lowest visible part of the water column attached to an HRT boiler should be AT LEAST
   A. 3 inches above the top row of tubes
   B. 6 inches above the fusible plug
   C. 1 inch above the top row of tubes
   D. ½ inch above the fusible plug

2. The function of a fusible plug is to
   A. melt if the water temperature is too high
   B. prevent too high a furnace temperature
   C. prevent excessive steam pressure from developing in the boiler
   D. melt when the water level drops below the level of the plug

3. To control the temperature of water in a domestic water supply tank, the device used is USUALLY a
   A. thermostat
   B. pressuretrol
   C. solenoid valve
   D. aquastat

4. A house trap is a device placed in the house drain immediately inside the foundation wall of the building.
   Its MAIN purpose is to
   A. trap sediment flowing in the house drain to the street sewer
   B. prevent sewer gases from circulating in the building plumbing system
   C. maintain air pressure balance in the vent lines of the plumbing system
   D. provide a means for cleaning the waste lines of the plumbing system

5. In the care and operation of steam boilers, a procedure that is considered GOOD practice is to
   A. open the safety valve in the event low water is found
   B. refill the boiler with cold water when the boiler is hot
   C. remove the boiler from service immediately if the water level cannot be determined because the gauge glass is broken
   D. use hot water where possible in refilling a boiler prior to firing

6. The addition of moisture to coal to promote combustion of coal is commonly referred to as
   A. tempering   B. dusting   C. watering   D. dehumidifying

7. The purpose of fire doors in a building is to
   A. prevent fires
   B. prevent arson
   C. avoid panic
   D. prevent the spread of fire

8. Of the following, the type of fire extinguisher that is MOST satisfactory for use on a fire in a place of operating electrical equipment is
   A. carbon dioxide
   B. sand pail
   C. soda acid
   D. foam

9. The device which is LEAST likely to be used by the custodian in cleaning minor stoppages in the plumbing system is a
   A. snake   B. auger   C. plunger   D. trowel

10. The PROPER cleaning agent for a paint brush that has been used to shellac a floor is
    A. gasoline   B. linseed oil   C. alcohol   D. turpentine

11. In cutting the ends of a number of lengths of wood at an angle of 45°, one would PREFERABLY use a
    A. protractor
    B. triangle
    C. miter box
    D. movable head T-square

12. To the custodian, the term *zeolite* refers to
    A. boiler insulation
    B. combustion chamber refractories
    C. boiler tube cleaning agent
    D. boiler water softening

13. A custodian notices a man in a corridor of the building. This visitor identifies himself as a police officer and states that he is observing a student in one of the classes.
    The custodian
    A. make no further inquiry of the police officer
    B. ask the police officer to check with the school principal if he has not already done so
    C. ask for all details, the name of the student, and reason for observation so that he can report the visit in his log book
    D. ask the police officer to leave the building unless he has received permission from the Board of Education in writing

14. When a paint coat blisters, the cause is USUALLY:
    A. Paint coat is too thick
    B. Plaster pores not sealed properly
    C. Moisture under the paint coat
    D. Too much oil in paint

15. Galvanized iron pails resist rusting because the surface of the iron is coated with
    A. copper   B. zinc   C. aluminum   D. lead

16. To maintain brick walls and to eliminate or prevent leaks, the walls are USUALLY
    A. painted   B. sprayed   C. pointed   D. refaced

17. A safety device that can be used instead of a fuse to protect a piece of electrical equipment is a
    A. circuit breaker
    B. rheostat
    C. toggle switch
    D. relay

18. Custodians are required to abide by snow removal regulations, which state that snow be removed
    A. from sidewalks within four hours after snow ceases to fall during daytime
    B. from sidewalks within 24 hours after snowfall ceases
    C. within a reasonable period only from walks immediately in front of school entrances
    D. from sidewalks within 12 hours only if the fall is greater than four inches

19. Which of the following types of grates should be used for ease in cleaning fires when hand firing large boilers under natural draft at heavy loads with #1 buckwheat?
    A. Dumping grates
    B. Stationary grates with ¾" air spaces
    C. Stationary grates (pinhole type)
    D. Shaking grates

20. Which of the following fuels contains the GREATEST number of heat units per pound?
    A. Hard coal
    B. #6 fuel oil
    C. Yard screenings
    D. Bituminous coal

21. The purpose of admitting air over the fire in a coal-fired furnace is USUALLY to
    A. reduce the stack gases temperature
    B. improve the draft
    C. reduce the smoke
    D. reduce the draft

22. In most usual types of large capacity oil burners using #6 oil, under fully automatic control, the atomization of the oil is produced by the
    A. pressure from the pump
    B. pressure from the secondary air fan
    C. oil temperature from the heater
    D. rotation of the burner assembly by the motor

23. Which of the following comes the closest to indicating the number of degree-days in a normal heating season in New York City?
    A. 3000   B. 4000   C. 5000   D. 6000

24. A badly sooted HRT boiler under coal firing will show a ____ than a clean boiler.
    A. higher CO_2 value
    B. lower CO_2 value
    C. higher stack temperature
    D. lower draft loss

25. The direct room radiator in a school with a pneumatically controlled steam heating system is cold, while the adjoining rooms are heated adequately.
Of the following, the FIRST thing you would check in the room is the
   A. steam pipe in the room before the pneumatic steam valve
   B. thermostat
   C. pneumatic steam valve
   D. thermostatic trap

26. A vaporstat used on a fully automatic heavy oil burning rotary cup installation, with separate motor driven oil pump, is GENERALLY used to
   A. keep the boiler pressure within proper limits
   B. regulate the pressure of the primary air
   C. regulate the pressure of the secondary air
   D. shut down the burner when primary air failure occurs

27. Suppose that a small oil fire has broken out in the boiler room of your building.
Of the following, the one that is LEAST suitable as an extinguisher is
   A. soda acid   B. pyrene (carbon tetra chloride
   C. foamite   D. carbon dioxide

28. An electric elevator car stalls on the ground floor of a school building.
Of the following, the item you would be LEAST likely to check in your inspection is
   A. *baby switch*   B. floor door switch
   C. limit switch   D. current to elevator motors

29. In an investigation of a complaint of sewer gas from a urinal in a regularly used toilet room, you find that the trap seal has been lost.
The LEAST common cause of this condition is
   A. evaporation of water from the trap
   B. vent blocked up
   C. high wind over roof vent
   D. self-siphonage

30. Of the following, the cleaning assignment which you would LEAST prefer to have performed during school hours is
   A. sweeping of corridors and stairs
   B. cleaning and polishing brass fixtures
   C. cleaning toilets
   D. dusting of offices, halls, and special rooms

31. BEST combustion conditions exist when the stack haze as indicated on the Ringelman chart scale is Number
   A. 1   B. 3   C. 5   D. 6

32. A pop safety valve is commonly a
   A. member with a rupture section   B. dead weight valve
   C. ball and lever valve   D. spring-loaded valve

33. Fusible plugs used as protective devices in HRT boilers producing low pressure steam should melt at temperatures
    A. above the temperature of the steam and below the temperature of the flue gases
    B. at the same temperature as the steam
    C. above the usual temperature of both the flue gases and the steam
    D. at about the same temperature as the flue gases

34. The high low water alarm of a steam boiler is USUALLY located in the
    A. boiler
    B. gauge glass
    C. water column
    D. feedwater

35. What is an advantage of shaking grates over stationary grates?
    A. The fire can be cleaned without opening the fire door.
    B. They are warp-proof.
    C. They are usually more sturdily constructed than stationary grates.
    D. Deeper firebed can usually be maintained.

36. An ACCEPTABLE method of detecting air leaks in the setting of a boiler is
    A. placing an open flame or burning torch near the point where the leaks are suspected
    B. coating the suspected parts of the setting with heavy grease
    C. coating the suspected points of leakage with a heavy soap emulsion
    D. inspecting suspected areas of leakage with a powerful light and hand magnifier

37. In a plumbing installation, an escutcheon is a
    A. metal collar
    B. reducing tee
    C. valve
    D. single sweep

38. A leaking faucet system can be repaired by replacing the
    A. flange or the seat
    B. nipple
    C. o-ring or the packing
    D. cock

39. The abbreviation O.S. and Y, as used in plumbing, apply to a(n)
    A. hot well   B. radiator   C. injector   D. gate valve

40. Gas range piping should have a MINIMUM diameter of _____ inch.
    A. ¾   B. ½   C. ¼   D. ⅛

KEY (CORRECT ANSWERS)

1.	A	11.	C	21.	C	31.	A
2.	D	12.	D	22.	D	32.	D
3.	D	13.	B	23.	C	33.	B
4.	B	14.	C	24.	C	34.	C
5.	C	15.	B	25.	A	35.	A
6.	A	16.	C	26.	D	36.	A
7.	D	17.	A	27.	A	37.	A
8.	A	18.	A	28.	C	38.	C
9.	D	19.	A	29.	A	39.	D
10.	C	20.	B	30.	D	40.	A

EXAMINATION SECTION
TEST 1

DIRECTIONS: Each question or incomplete statement is followed by several suggested answers or completions. Select the one that BEST answers the question or completes the statement. *PRINT THE LETTER OF THE CORRECT ANSWER IN THE SPACE AT THE RIGHT.*

Questions 1-5.

DIRECTIONS: Column I lists cleaning jobs. Column II lists cleaning agents and devices. Select the PROPER cleansing agent from Column II for each job in Column I. Place the letter of the cleansing agent selected in the space at the right corresponding to the number of the cleaning job.

COLUMN I		COLUMN II	
1.	Chewing gum	A. Muriatic acid	1.____
2.	Ink stains	B. Broad bladed knife	2.____
3.	Fingermarks on glass	C. Kerosene	3.____
4.	Rust stains on porcelain	D. Oxalic acid	4.____
5.	Hardened dirt on porcelain	E. Lye	5.____
		F. Linseed oil	

6. When the bristles of a floor brush have worn short, the brush should be 6.____
   A. thrown away and the handles saved
   B. saved and the brush used on rough cement floors
   C. saved and used for high dusting in classrooms
   D. saved and used for the weekly scrubbing of linoleum floors

7. Feather dusters should NOT be used because they 7.____
   A. take more time to use than other dusters
   B. cannot be cleaned
   C. do not take up the dust but merely move it from one place to another
   D. do not stir up the dust and streak the furniture with dust rails

8. Floors that are usually NOT waxed are those made of 8.____
   A. pine wood   B. mastic tile   C. rubber tile   D. terrazzo

9. For sweeping under radiators and other inaccessible places, the MOST appropriate tool is the 9.____
   A. counter brush   B. dry mop
   C. feather duster   D. 16" floor brush

10. A cleansing agent that should NOT be used in the cleaning of windows is
    A. water containing fine pumice
    B. water containing a small amount of ammonia
    C. water containing a little kerosene
    D. a paste cleanser made from water and cleaning powder

11. The BEST way to dust desks is to use a
    A. circular motion with soft dry cloth that has been washed
    B. damp cloth, taking care not to disturb papers on the desk
    C. soft cloth, moistened with oil, using a back and forth motion
    D. back and forth motion with a soft dry cloth

12. Trisodium phosphate is a substance BEST used in
    A. washing kalsomined walls
    B. polishing of brass
    C. washing mastic tile floors
    D. clearing stoppages

13. Treated linoleum is PROPERLY cleaned by daily
    A. dusting with a treated mop
    B. sweeping with a floor brush
    C. mopping with a weak soap solution
    D. mopping after removal of dust with a floor brush

14. Of the following, the MOST proper use of chamois skin is
    A. drying of window glass after washing
    B. washing of window glass
    C. polishing of metal fixtures
    D. drying toilet bowls after washing

15. A squeegee is a tool which is used in
    A. cleaning stoppages in waste lines
    B. the central vacuum cleaning system
    C. cleaning inside boiler surfaces
    D. drying windows after washing

16. Concrete and cement floors are usually painted a battleship gray color. The MOST important reason for painting the floor is
    A. to improve the appearance of the floor
    B. the paint prevents the absorption of too much water when the floor is mopped
    C. the paint makes the floor safer and less slippery
    D. the concrete becomes harder and will not settle

17. A resin-base floor finish USUALLY
    A. gives the highest lustre of all floor finishes
    B. should be applied in one heavy coat
    C. provides a slip-resistant surface
    D. should not be used on asphalt tile

18. The one of the following cleaning operations on soft floors that generally requires MOST NEARLY the same amount of time per 1,000 square feet as damp mopping is
    A. applying a thin coat of wax
    B. sweeping
    C. dust mopping
    D. wet mopping

18.____

19. Of the following cleaning jobs, the one that should be allowed the MOST time to complete a 1,000 square foot area is
    A. vacuuming carpets
    B. washing painted walls
    C. stripping and waxing soft floors
    D. machine-scrubbing hard floors

19.____

20. When instructing your staff in the use of sodium silicate, you should tell them that it is MOST commonly used to
    A. seal concrete floors
    B. condition leather
    C. treat boiler water
    D. neutralize acid wastes

20.____

21. Cleaners should be instructed that dust mopping is LEAST appropriate for removing light soil from _____ floors.
    A. terrazzo
    B. unsealed concrete
    C. resin-finished soft
    D. sealed wood

21.____

22. Of the following, the substance that should be recommended for polishing hardwood furniture is
    A. lemon oil polish
    B. neatsfoot oil
    C. paste wax
    D. water-emulsion wax

22.____

23. The use of concentrated acid to remove stains from ceramic tile bathroom floors USUALLY results in making the surface
    A. pitted and porous
    B. clean and shiny
    C. harder and glossier
    D. waterproof

23.____

24. Asphalt tile floors should be protected by coating with
    A. hard-milled soap
    B. water-emulsion wax
    C. sodium metaphosphate
    D. varnish

24.____

25. Of the following, the BEST way to economize on cleaning tools and materials is to
    A. train the cleaners to use them properly
    B. order at least a three-year supply of every item in order to avoid annual price increases
    C. attach a price sticker to every item so that the people using them will realize their high cost
    D. delay ordering material for three months at the beginning of each year to be sure that the old material is used to the fullest extent

25.____

KEY (CORRECT ANSWERS)

1.	B		11.	D
2.	D		12.	C
3.	C		13.	A
4.	A		14.	A
5.	C		15.	D
6.	B		16.	B
7.	C		17.	C
8.	D		18.	A
9.	A		19.	C
10.	A		20.	A

21. B
22. C
23. A
24. B
25. A

TEST 2

DIRECTIONS: Each question or incomplete statement is followed by several suggested answers or completions. Select the one that BEST answers the question or completes the statement. *PRINT THE LETTER OF THE CORRECT ANSWER IN THE SPACE AT THE RIGHT.*

1. Of the following office cleaning jobs performed during the year, the one which should be done MOST frequently is
   A. cleaning the fluorescent lights
   B. dusting the Venetian blinds
   C. cleaning the bookcase glass
   D. carpetsweeping the rug

   1.____

2. The BEST polishing agent to use on wood furniture is
   A. pumice
   B. paste wax
   C. water emulsion wax
   D. neatsfoot oil

   2.____

3. Lemon oil polish is used BEST to polish
   A. exterior bronze
   B. marble walls
   C. leather seats
   D. lacquered metal

   3.____

4. Cleaning with trisodium phosphate is MOST likely to damage
   A. toilet bowls
   B. drain pipes
   C. polished marble floors
   D. rubber tile floors

   4.____

5. Of the following cleaning agents, the one which should NOT be used to remove stains from urinals is
   A. caustic lye   B. detergent   C. oxalic acid   D. muriatic acid

   5.____

6. The one of the following cleaners which GENERALLY contains an abrasive is
   A. caustic lye
   B. trisodium phosphate
   C. scouring powder
   D. ammonia

   6.____

7. The instructions on a box of cleaning powder say: *Mix one pound of cleaning powder in four gallons of water.*
   According to these instructions, how many ounces of cleaning powder should be mixed in one gallon of water?
   A. 4   B. 8   C. 12   D. 16

   7.____

8. In accordance with recommended practice, a dust mop, when not being used, should be stored
   A. hanging, handle end down
   B. hanging, handle end up
   C. standing on the floor, handle end down
   D. standing on the floor, handle end up

   8.____

9. The two types of floors found in public buildings are classified as hard floors and soft floors. 9.____
 An example of a hard floor is one made of
 A. linoleum B. cork C. ceramic tile D. asphalt tile

10. A squeegee is a tool that is MAINLY used to clean 10.____
 A. painted walls
 B. radiator covers
 C. window glass
 D. ceramic tile floors

11. The BEST way to determine whether a cleaner is doing his work well is by 11.____
 A. observing the cleaner at work for several hours
 B. asking the cleaner questions about his work
 C asking other cleaners to rate his work
 D. inspecting the cleanliness of the spaces assigned to the cleaner

12. The PRIMARY purpose of using a disinfectant material is to 12.____
 A. kill germs
 B. destroy odors
 C. remove stains
 D. kill insects

13. Windows should be washed by using a solution of warm water mixed with 13.____
 A. chlorine bleach
 B. kerosene
 C. ammonia
 D. soft soap

14. Of the following, the MOST effective way to reduce waste of cleaning tools is to 14.____
 A. keep careful records of how often tools are issued
 B. require that the old tool be returned before issuing a new one
 C. require that all tools be used for a fixed number of hours before replacing them
 D. train the cleaners to use the tools properly

15. The number of square feet of unobstructed corridor floor space that a cleaner should sweep in an hour is MOST NEARLY 15.____
 A. 1200 B. 2400 C. 4000 D. 6000

16. Sweeping compound is used on concrete floors MAINLY to 16.____
 A. polish the floor
 B. keep the dust down
 C. soften the encrusted dirt
 D. provide a non-slip surface

17. The BEST attachment to use on an electric scrubbing machine when stripping waxed resilient flooring is a 17.____
 A. nylon disk
 B. soft brush
 C. steel wool pad
 D. pumice wheel

18. A counter brush is BEST suited to cleaning 18.____
 A. water cooler drains
 B. radiators
 C. light fixtures
 D. lavatory fixtures

19. In high dusting of walls and ceilings, the CORRECT procedure is to
    A. begin with lower walls and process up to the ceiling
    B. remove pictures and window shades only if they are dusty
    C. clean the windows thoroughly before dusting any other part of the room
    D. begin with the ceiling, then dust the walls

20. When cleaning a room, the cleaner should
    A. dust desks before sweeping
    B. dust desks after sweeping
    C. open windows wide during the desk dusting process
    D. begin dusting at rows most distant from entrance door

21. Too much water on asphalt tile is objectionable MAINLY because the tile
    A. will tend to become discolored or spotted
    B. may be loosened from the floor
    C. will be softened and made uneven
    D. colors will tend to run

22. To reduce the slip hazard resulting from waxing linoleum, the MOST practical of the following methods is
    A. apply the wax in one heavy coat
    B. apply the wax after varnishing the linoleum
    C. buff the wax surface thoroughly
    D. apply the wax in several thin coats

23. Assume that the water emulsion wax needed for routine waxing in your building is 15 gallons per month. This wax is supplied in 55-gallon drums.
    To cover your needs for a year, the MINIMUM number of drums you would have to request is
    A. two   B. three   C. four   D. six

24. In washing down the walls, the correct procedure is to start at the bottom of the wall and work to the top.
    The MOST important reason for this is:
    A. Dirt streaking will tend to be avoided or easily removed
    B. Less cleansing agent will be required
    C. Rinse water will not be required
    D. The time for cleaning the wall is less than if washing at the top of the wall

25. In mopping a wood floor, the cleaner should
    A. mop against the grain of the wood wherever possible
    B. mop as large an area as possible at one time
    C. wet the floor before mopping with a cleaning agent
    D. mop only aisles and clear areas and use a scrub brush under desks and chairs

KEY (CORRECT ANSWERS)

1. D
2. B
3. A
4. C
5. D

6. C
7. A
8. B
9. C
10. C

11. D
12. A
13. C
14. D
15. D

16. B
17. A
18. B
19. D
20. B

21. B
22. D
23. C
24. A
25. C

TEST 3

DIRECTIONS: Each question or incomplete statement is followed by several suggested answers or completions. Select the one that BEST answers the question or completes the statement. *PRINT THE LETTER OF THE CORRECT ANSWER IN THE SPACE AT THE RIGHT.*

1. The MAIN reason for using a sweeping compound is to 1._____
   A. spot-finish waxed surfaces
   B. retard dust when sweeping floors
   C. loosen accumulations of grease
   D. remove paint spots from the flooring

2. The one of the following cleaning agents which is recommended for use on marble floors is 2._____
   A. an acid cleaner
   B. a soft soap
   C. trisodium phosphate
   D. a neutral liquid detergent

3. A cleaning solution of one cup of soap chips dissolved in a pail of warm water can be used to wash 3._____
   A. painted walls
   B. rubber tile
   C. marble walls
   D. terrazzo floors

4. Sodium fluoride is a 4._____
   A. pesticide   B. disinfectant   C. detergent   D. paint thinner

5. Scratches or burns in linoleum, rubber tile, or cork floors should be removed by rubbing with 5._____
   A. crocus cloth
   B. fine steel wool
   C. sandpaper
   D. emery cloth

6. A room 12 feet wide by 25 feet long has a floor area of _____ square feet. 6._____
   A. 37   B. 200   C. 300   D. 400

7. A cleaning solution should be applied to a painted wall using a 7._____
   A. wool rag   B. brush   C. sponge   D. squeegee

8. When scrubbing a wooden floor, it is ADVISABLE to 8._____
   A. flood the surface with the cleaning solution in order to float the dirt out of all cracks and crevices
   B. hose off the loosened dirt before starting the scrubbing operation
   C. pick up the cleaning solution as soon as possible
   D. mix a mild acid with the cleaning solution in order to clean the surface quickly

9. How many hours will it take a worker to sweep a floor space of 2800 square feet if he sweeps at the pace of 800 square feet per hour? 9._____
   A. 8   B. 6½   C. 3½   D. 2½

10. One gallon of water contains
    A. 2 quarts   B. 4 quarts   C. 2 pints   D. 4 pints

11. A standard cleaning solution is prepared by mixing 4 ounces of detergent powder in 2 gallons of water.
    The number of ounces of detergent powder needed for the same strength solution in 5 gallons of water is
    A. 4   B. 6   C. 8   D. 10

12. The principal reason why soap should NOT be used in cleaning windows is
    A. it causes loosening of the putty
    B. it may cause rotting of the wood frames
    C. a film is left on the window, requiring additional rinsing
    D. frequent use of soap will cause the glass to become permanently clouded

13. When a window pane is broken, the FIRST step the custodian takes is to
    A. remove broken glass from floors and the window sill
    B. determine the cause
    C. remove the putty with a putty knife
    D. prepare a piece of glass to replace the broken pane

14. Your instructions to a cleaner about the proper sweeping of offices should include the following instruction:
    A. Do not move chairs and wastebaskets from their places when sweeping
    B. Place chairs and baskets on the desks to get them out of the way
    C. Set aside the loose small furniture and chairs in an orderly manner when sweeping office floors
    D. Move the desks and chairs to the side of the room close to the wall in order to sweep properly

15. To remove dirt accumulations after the completion of the sweeping task, brushes should be
    A. tapped on the floor in the normal sweeping position
    B. struck on the floor against the side of the block
    C. struck on the floor against the end of the block
    D. turned upside down and the handle tapped on the floor

16. To sweep rough cement floors in a basement, the BEST tool to use is a
    A. deck brush   B. new 30" floor brush
    C. corn broom   D. treated mop

17. When a floor is scrubbed, it is NOT correct to
    A. use a steady, even rotary motion
    B. rinse the floor with clean hot water
    C. have the mop strokes follow the boards when drying the floor
    D. wet the floor first by pouring several bucketsful of water on it

18. Flushing with a hose is MOST appropriate as a method of cleaning
    A. terrazzo floors of corridors
    B. untreated wood floors
    C. linoleum floors where not in frequent use
    D. cement floors

19. Improper use of a carbon dioxide type portable fire extinguisher may cause injury to the operator because
    A. handling the nozzle during discharge can cause frostbite to the skin
    B. carbon dioxide is highly poisonous if breathed into the lungs
    C. use of carbon dioxide on an oil fire can cause a chemical explosion
    D. the powdery residue left by the discharge is highly caustic to the skin

20. When using a portable single ladder with ten rungs, the GREATEST number of rungs that a cleaner should climb up is
    A. 7   B. 8   C. 9   D. 10

21. Of the following types of portable fire extinguishers, the one which should be used to control a fire in or around live electrical equipment is the _____ type.
    A. foam
    B. soda acid
    C. carbon dioxide
    D. gas cartridge water

22. The MOST frequent cause of accidental injuries to workers on the job is
    A. unsafe working practices of employees
    B. poor design of buildings and working areas
    C. lack of warning signs in hazardous work areas
    D. lack of adequate safety guards on equipment and machinery

23. Of the following, the MOST important purpose of preparing an accident report on an injury to a cleaner is to help
    A. collect statistics on different types of accidents
    B. calm the feelings of the injured cleaner
    C. prevent similar accidents in the future
    D. prove that the cleaner was at fault

24. The one of the following types of locks that is used on emergency exit doors is the
    A. panic   B. dead   C. cinch   D. toggle

25. The one of the following types of locks that USUALLY contains both a live volt and a dead bolt is a _____ lock.
    A. mortise
    B. double-hung window
    C. loose pin butt
    D. window frame

KEY (CORRECT ANSWERS)

1.	B	11.	D
2.	D	12.	C
3.	A	13.	A
4.	A	14.	C
5.	B	15.	A
6.	C	16.	C
7.	C	17.	D
8.	C	18.	D
9.	C	19.	A
10.	B	20.	B

21. C
22. A
23. C
24. A
25. A

EXAMINATION SECTION
TEST 1

DIRECTIONS: Each question or incomplete statement is followed by several suggested answers or completions. Select the one that BEST answers the question or completes the statement. *PRINT THE LETTER OF THE CORRECT ANSWER IN THE SPACE AT THE RIGHT.*

1. If you can't come to work in the morning because you do not feel well, you should

    A. call your supervisor and let him know that you are sick
    B. try to get someone else to take your place
    C. have your doctor call your office as proof that you are sick
    D. come to work anyway so that you won't lose your job

    1._____

2. Many machines have certain safety devices for the operators.
   The MOST important reason for having these safety devices is to

    A. increase the amount of work that the machines can do
    B. permit repairs to be made on the machines without shutting them down
    C. help prevent accidents to people who use the machines
    D. reduce the cost of electric power needed to run the machines

    2._____

3. While working on the job, you accidentally break a window pane. No one is around, and you are able to clean up the broken pieces of glass.
   It would then be BEST for you to

    A. leave a note near the window that a new glass has to be put in because it was accidentally broken
    B. forget about the whole thing because the window was not broken on purpose
    C. write a report to your supervisor telling him that you saw a broken window pane that has to be fixed
    D. tell your supervisor that you accidentally broke the window pane while working

    3._____

4. There is a two-light fixture in the room where you are working. One of the light bulbs goes out, and you need more light to work by.
   You should

    A. change the fuse in the fuse box
    B. have a new bulb put in
    C. call for an electrician and stop work until he comes
    D. find out what is causing the short circuit

    4._____

5. The BEST way to remove some small pieces of broken glass from a floor is to

    A. use a brush and dust pan
    B. pick up the pieces carefully with your hands
    C. use a wet mop and a wringer
    D. sweep the pieces into the corner of the room

    5._____

6. When you are not sure about some instructions that your supervisor has given you on how to do a certain job, it would be BEST for you to

   A. start doing the work and stop when you come to the part that you do not understand
   B. ask the supervisor to go over the instructions which are not clear to you
   C. do the job immediately from beginning to the end, leaving out the part that you are not sure of
   D. wait until the supervisor leaves and then ask a more experienced worker to explain the job to you

7. When an employee first comes on the job, he is given a period of training by his supervisor.
   The MAIN reason for this training period is to

   A. make sure that the employee will learn to do his work correctly and safely
   B. give the employee a chance to show the supervisor that he can learn quickly
   C. allow the supervisor and the employee a chance to become friendly with each other
   D. find out which employees will make good supervisors later on

8. After you open a sealed box of supplies, you find that the box is not full and that some of the supplies are missing.
   You should

   A. use fewer supplies than you intended to
   B. seal the box and take it back to the storeroom
   C. get signed statements from other employees that when you opened the box, it was not full
   D. tell your supervisor about it

9. Suppose that after you have been on the job a few months, your supervisor shows you some small mistakes you are making in your work.
   You should

   A. tell your supervisor that these mistakes don't keep you from finishing your work
   B. ask your supervisor how you can avoid these mistakes
   C. try to show your supervisor that your way of doing the work is just as good as his way of doing it
   D. check with the other workers to find out if your supervisor is also finding fault with them

10. If your supervisor gives you an order to do a special job which you do not like to do, you should

    A. take a long time to do the job so that you won't get this job again
    B. do the job the best way you know how even though you don't like it
    C. make believe that you didn't hear your supervisor and do your regular work
    D. say nothing but tell another employee that the supervisor wants him to do this special job

11. If two employees who are working together on a job do not agree on how to do the job, it would be BEST

    A. for each worker to do the job in his own way until it is finished
    B. to put off doing the job until both workers agree to do it the same way
    C. to ask the supervisor to decide on the way the job is to be done
    D. for each worker to ask for a transfer to another assignment because they can't get along with each other

11.____

12. Suppose that in order to finish your work, you have to lift a heavy box off the floor onto an empty desk.
    You should

    A. leave the box where it is and tell your supervisor that you have finished your work
    B. lift the box by yourself very quickly so that your supervisor will see that you are a strong, willing worker
    C. ask another employee to give you a hand to lift the box off the floor
    D. complain to your supervisor that he should check a job before giving you such a tough assignment

12.____

13. Bulletin boards for the posting of official notices are usually put up near the place where employees check in and out each day.
    For an employee to spend a few minutes each day to read the new notices is

    A. *good;* these notices give him information about the Department and his own work
    B. *bad;* all important information is given to employees by their supervisors
    C. *good;* this is a way to "take a break" during the day
    D. *bad;* the notices can't help him in his work

13.____

14. Suppose that your supervisor gives you a job to do and tells you that he wants you to finish it in three hours.
    If you finish the work at the end of 2 hours, you should

    A. wait until the three hours are up and then tell your supervisor that you are finished
    B. go to your supervisor and tell him that you finished a half-hour ahead of time
    C. spend the next half-hour getting ready for the next job you think your supervisor may give you
    D. take a half-hour rest period because good work deserves a reward

14.____

15. Which one of the following is it LEAST important to include in an accident report?

    A. Name and address of the injured person
    B. Date, time, and place where the accident happened
    C. Name and address of the injured person's family doctor
    D. An explanation of how the accident happened

15.____

16. If, near the end of the day, you realize that you made a mistake in your work and you can't do the work over, you should

    A. forget about it because there is only a small chance that the mistake can be traced back to you
    B. wait a few days and take the blame for the mistake if it is caught
    C. ask the other employees to keep the mistake a secret so that no one can be blamed
    D. tell your supervisor about the mistake right away

16.____

17. Employees should wipe up water spilled on floors immediately.
The BEST reason for this is that water on a floor

   A. is a sign that employees are sloppy
   B. makes for a slippery condition that could cause an accident
   C. will eat into the wax protecting the floor
   D. is against health regulations

18. Another worker, who is a good friend of yours, leaves work an hour before quitting time to take care of a personal matter. When you leave later, you find that your friend did not sign out on the timesheet.
For you to sign out for your friend would be

   A. *good*, because he will do the same for you some day when you want to leave early
   B. *bad*, because other employees will also want you to do the same favor for them on other days
   C. *good*, because the timesheet should not have any empty spaces on it
   D. *bad*, because timesheets are official records which employees should keep honestly and accurately

19. While you are working, a person asks you how to get to an office which you know is one floor above you in the building where you work.
It would be BEST for you to tell this person that

   A. you can't answer any questions because you have to finish your work
   B. he should go back to the lobby and check the list of offices
   C. the office he is looking for is on the next floor
   D. he should call the office he is looking for to get exact instructions on how to get there

20. While you are at work, you find a sealed brown envelope under a desk. The envelope is marked *Personal - Hand Delivery* and is addressed to an official who has an office in the building where you are working.
You should

   A. drop the envelope into the nearest mailbox so that it can be delivered the next day
   B. look up the telephone number of the official and call him up to tell him what you have found
   C. put the envelope in your pocket and come in early the next day to deliver it personally to the official
   D. give the envelope to your supervisor right away and tell him where you found it

21. A messenger delivered 32 letters on Monday, 47 on Tuesday, 29 on Wednesday, 36 on Thursday, and 41 on Friday.
How many letters did he deliver altogether?

   A. 157   B. 185   C. 218   D. 229

22. Mr. White paid 4% sales tax on a $95 television set.
The amount of sales tax that he paid was

   A. $9.50   B. $4.00   C. $3.80   D. $.95

23. How many square feet are there in a room which is 25 feet long and 35 feet wide? 23.____
    _____ square feet.
    A. 600   B. 750   C. 875   D. 925

24. How much would it cost to send a 34 pound package by parcel post if the postage is 24.____
    $1.60 for the first 20 pounds and 7 for each additional pound?
    A. $2.34   B. $2.58   C. $2.66   D. $2.80

25. Adding together 1/2, 3/4, and 1/8, the total is 25.____
    A. 1 1/4   B. 1 1/2   C. 1 3/8   D. 1 3/4

26. If a piece of wood 40 inches long is cut into two pieces so that the larger piece is three 26.____
    times as long as the, smaller piece, the smaller piece is _____ inches.
    A. 4   B. 5   C. 8   D. 10

27. Two friends, Smith and Jones, together spend $1,800 to buy a car. 27.____
    If Smith put up twice as much money as Jones, then Jones' share of the cost of the car was
    A. $300   B. $600   C. $900   D. $1,200

28. In a certain agency, two-thirds of the employees are clerks and the remainder are typists. 28.____
    If there are 180 clerks, then the number of typists in this agency is
    A. 270   B. 90   C. 240   D. 60

Questions 29-35.

DIRECTIONS: Answer Questions 29 through 35 ONLY according to the information given in the chart below.

EMPLOYEE RECORD

Name of Employee	Where Assigned	Number of Days Absent Vacation	Sick Leave	Yearly Salary
Carey	Laundry	18	4	$18,650
Hayes	Mortuary	24	8	$17,930
Irwin	Buildings	20	17	$18,290
King	Supply	12	10	$17,930
Lane	Mortuary	17	8	$17,750
Martin	Buildings	13	12	$17,750
Prince	Buildings	5	7	$17,750
Quinn	Supply	19	0	$17,250
Sands	Buildings	23	10	$18,470
Victor	Laundry	21	2	$18,150

29. The *only* employee who was NOT absent because of sickness is   29.___
    A. Hayes   B. Lane   C. Victor   D. Quinn

30. The employee with the HIGHEST salary is   30.___
    A. Carey   B. Irwin   C. Sands   D. Victor

31. The employee with the LOWEST salary is assigned to the _____ Bureau.   31.___
    A. Laundry   B. Mortuary   C. Building   D. Supply

32. Which one of these was absent or on vacation more than 20 days?   32.___
    A. Irwin   B. Lane   C. Quinn   D. Victor

33. The number of employees whose salary is LESS than $18,100 a year is   33.___
    A. 4   B. 5   C. 6   D. 7

34. MOST employees are assigned to   34.___
    A. Laundry   B. Mortuary   C. Buildings   D. Supply

35. From the chart, you can figure out for each employee   35.___
    A. how long he has worked in his present assignment
    B. how many days vacation he has left
    C. how many times he has been late
    D. how much he earns a month

KEY (CORRECT ANSWERS)

1. A		16. D	
2. C		17. B	
3. D		18. D	
4. B		19. C	
5. A		20. D	
6. B		21. B	
7. A		22. C	
8. D		23. C	
9. B		24. B	
10. B		25. C	
11. C		26. D	
12. C		27. B	
13. A		28. B	
14. B		29. D	
15. C		30. A	

31. D
32. D
33. C
34. C
35. D

TEST 2

DIRECTIONS: Each question or incomplete statement is followed by several suggested answers or completions. Select the one that BEST answers the question or completes the statement. *PRINT THE LETTER OF THE CORRECT ANSWER IN THE SPACE AT THE RIGHT.*

Questions 1-5.

DIRECTIONS: Answer Questions 1 to 5 ONLY according to the information given in the following passage.

EMPLOYEE LEAVE REGULATIONS

Peter Smith, as a full-time permanent City employee under the Career and Salary Plan, earns an "annual leave allowance" This consists of a certain number of days off a year with pay and may be used for vacation, personal business, and for observing religious holidays. As a newly appointed employee, during his first eight years of City service, he will earn an "annual leave allowance" of twenty days off a year (an average of 1 2/3 days off a month). After he has finished eight full years of working for the City, he will begin earning an additional five days off a year. His "annual leave allowance," therefore, will then be twenty-five days a year and will remain at this amount for seven full years. He will begin earning an additional two days off a year after he has completed a total of fifteen years of City employment. Therefore, in his sixteenth year of working for the City, Mr. Smith will be earning twenty-seven days off a year as his "annual leave allowance" (an average of 2 1/4 days off a month).

A "sick leave allowance" of one day a month is also given to Mr. Smith, but it can be used only in case of actual illness. When Mr. Smith returns to work after using "sick leave allowance," he must have a doctor's note if the absence is for a total of more than three days, but he may also be required to show a doctor's note for absences of one, two, or three days.

1. According to the above passage, Mr. Smith's *annual leave allowance* consists of a certain number of days off a year which he

    A. does not get paid for
    B. gets paid for at time and a half
    C. may use for personal business
    D. may not use for observing religious holidays

    1.____

2. According to the above passage, after Mr. Smith has been working for the City for nine years, his *annual leave allowance* will be _____ days a year.

    A. 20   B. 25   C. 27   D. 37

    2.____

3. According to the above passage, Mr. Smith will begin earning an average of 2 1/4 days off a month as his *annual leave allowance* after he has worked for the City for _____ full years.

    A. 7   B. 8   C. 15   D. 17

    3.____

4. According to the above passage, Mr. Smith is given a *sick leave allowance* of

    A. 1 day every 2 months   B. 1 day per month
    C. 1 2/3 days per month   D. 2 1/4 days a month

    4.____

5. According to the above passage, when he uses *sick leave allowance*, Mr. Smith may be required to show a doctor's note

   A. even if his absence is for only 1 day
   B. only if his absence is for more than 2 days
   C. only if his absence is for more than 3 days
   D. only if his absence is for 3 days or more

Questions 6-9.

DIRECTIONS: Answer Questions 6 to 9 ONLY according to the information given in the following passag

MOPPING FLOORS

When mopping hardened cement floors, either painted or unpainted, a soap and water mixture should be used. This should be made by dissolving 1/2 a cup of soft soap in a pail of hot water. It is not desirable, however, under any circumstances, to use a soap and water mixture on cement floors that are not hardened. For mopping this type of floor, it is recommended that the cleaning agent be made up of two ounces of laundry soda mixed in a pail of water.

Soaps are not generally used on hard tile floors because slippery films may build up on the floor. It is generally recommended that these floors be mopped using a pail of hot water in which has been mixed two ounces of washing powder for each gallon of water. The floors should then be rinsed thoroughly.

After the mopping is finished, proper care should be taken of the mop. This is done by first cleaning the mop in clear, warm water. Then, it should be wrung out, after which the strands of the mop should be untangled. Finally, the mop should be hung by its handle to dry.

6. According to the above passage, you should NEVER use a soap and water mixture when mopping _____ floors.

   A. hardened cement   B. painted
   C. unhardened cement   D. unpainted

7. According to the above passage, using laundry soda mixed in a pail of water as a cleaning agent is recommended for

   A. all floors
   B. all floors except hard tile floors
   C. some cement floors
   D. lineoleum floor coverings only

8. According to the above passage, the generally recommended mixture for mopping hard tile floors is

   A. 1/2 a cup of soft soap for each gallon of hot water
   B. 1/2 a cup of soft soap in a pail of hot water
   C. 2 ounces of washing powder in a pail of hot water
   D. 2 ounces of washing powder for each gallon of hot water

9. According to the above passage, the proper care of a mop after it is used includes 9._____

   A. cleaning it in clear cold water and hanging it by its handle to dry
   B. wringing it out, untangling and drying it
   C. untangling its strands before wringing it out
   D. untangling its strands while cleaning it in clear water

Questions 10-13.

DIRECTIONS: Answer Questions 10 to 13 ONLY according to the information given in the following passage.

HANDLING HOSPITAL LAUNDRY

In a hospital, care must be taken when handling laundry in order to reduce the chance of germs spreading. There is always the possibility that dirty laundry will be carrying dangerous germs. To avoid catching germs when they are working with dirty laundry, laundry workers should be sure that any cuts or wounds they have are bandaged before they touch the dirty laundry. They should also be careful when handling this laundry not to rub their eyes, nose, or mout. Just like all other hospital workers, laundry workers should also protect themselves against germs by washing and rinsing their hands thoroughly before eating meals and before leaving work at the end of the day.

To be sure that germs from dirty laundry do not pass onto clean laundry and thereby increase the danger to patients, clean and dirty laundry should not be handled near each other or by the same person. Special care also has to be taken with laundry that comes from a patient who has a dangerous, highly contagious disease so that as few people as possible come in direct contact with this laundry. Laundry from this patient, therefore, should be kept separate from other dirty laundry at all times.

10. According to the above passage, when working with dirty laundry, laundry workers should 10._____

    A. destroy laundry carrying dangerous germs
    B. have any cuts bandaged before touching the dirty laundry
    C. never touch the dirty laundry directly
    D. rub their eyes, nose, and mouth to protect them from germs

11. According to the above passage, all hospital workers should wash their hands thoroughly 11._____

    A. after eating meals to remove any trace of food from their hands
    B. at every opportunity to show good example to the patients
    C. before eating meals to protect themselves against germs
    D. before starting work in the morning to feel fresh and ready to do a good day's work

12. According to the above passage, the danger to patients will increase 12._____

    A. unless a worker handles dirty and clean laundry at the same time
    B. unless clean and dirty laundry are handled near each other
    C. when clean laundry is ironed frequently
    D. when germs pass from dirty laundry to clean laundry

13. According to the above passage, laundry from a patient with a dangerous, highly contagious disease should be

    A. given special care so that as few people as possible come in direct contact with it
    B. handled in the same way as any other dirty laundry
    C. washed by hand
    D. separated from the other dirty laundry just before it is washed

Questions 14-17.

DIRECTIONS: Answer Questions 14 to 17 ONLY according to the information given in the following passage.

EMPLOYEE SUGGESTIONS

To increase the effectiveness of the New York City governments the City asks its employees to offer suggestions when they feel an improvement could be made in some government operation. The Employees' Suggestions Program was started to encourage City employees to do this. Through this Program, which is only for City employees, cash awards may be given to those whose suggestions are submitted and approve Suggestions are looked for not only from supervisors but from all City employees as any City employee may get an idea which might be approved and contribute greatly to the solution of some problem of City government.

Therefore, all suggestions for improvement are welcome, whether they be suggestions on how to improve working conditions, or on how to increase the speed with which work is done, or on how to reduce or eliminate such things as waste, time losses, accidents, or fire hazards. There are, however, a few types of suggestions for which cash awards can not be given. An example of this type would be a suggestion to increase salaries or a suggestion to change the regulations about annual leave or about sick leave. The number of suggestions sent in has increased sharply during the past few years. It is hoped that it will keep increasing in the future in order to meet the City's needs for more ideas for improved ways of doing things.

14. According to the above passage, the main reason why the City asks its employees for suggestions about government operations is to

    A. increase the effectiveness of the City government
    B. show that the Employees' Suggestion Program is working well
    C. show that everybody helps run the City government
    D. have the employee win a prize

15. According to the above passage, the Employees' Suggestion Program can approve awards only for those suggestions that come from

    A. City employees
    B. City employees who are supervisors
    C. City employees who are not supervisors
    D. experienced employees of the City

16. According to the above passage, a cash award can not be given through the Employees' Suggestion Program for a suggestion about 16._____

    A. getting work done faster
    B. helping prevent accidents on the job
    C. increasing the amount of annual leave for City employees
    D. reducing the chance of fire where City employees work

17. According to the above passage, the suggestions sent in during the past few years have 17._____

    A. all been approved
    B. generally been well written
    C. been mostly about reducing or eliminating waste
    D. been greater in number than before

Questions 18-21.

DIRECTIONS: Answer Questions 18 to 21 ONLY according to the information given in the following passage.

ACCIDENT PREVENTION

Many accidents and injuries can be prevented if employees learn to be more careful. The wearing of shoes with thin or badly worn soles or open toes can easily lead to foot injuries from tacks, nails, and chair and desk legs. Loose or torn clothing should not be worn near moving machinery. This is especially true of neckties which can very easily become caught in the machine. You should not place objects so that they block or partly block hallways, corridors, or other passageways. Even when they are stored in the proper place, tools, supplies, and equipment should be carefully placed or piled so as not to fall, nor have anything stick out from a pile. Before cabinets, lockers, or ladders are moved, the tops should be cleared of anything which might injure someone or fall of If necessary, use a dolly to move these or other bulky objects.

Despite all efforts to avoid accidents and injuries, however, some will happen. If an employee is injured, no matter how small the injury, he should report it to his supervisor and have the injury treated. A small cut that is not attended to can easily become infected and can cause more trouble than some injuries which at first seem more serious. It never pays to take chances.

18. According to the above passage, the one statement that is NOT true is that 18._____

    A. by being more careful, employees can reduce the number of accidents that happen
    B. women should wear shoes with open toes for comfort when working
    C. supplies should be piled so that nothing is sticking out from the pile
    D. if an employee sprains his wrist at work, he should tell his supervisor about it

19. According to the above passage, you should NOT wear loose clothing when you are 19._____

    A. in a corridor   B. storing tools
    C. opening cabinets   D. near moving machinery

20. According to the above passage, before moving a ladder, you should 20.___

    A. test all the rungs
    B. get a dolly to carry the ladder at all times
    C. remove everything from the top of the ladder which might fall off
    D. remove your necktie

21. According to the above passage, an employee who gets a slight cut should 21.___

    A. have it treated to help prevent infection
    B. know that a slight cut becomes more easily infected than a big cut
    C. pay no attention to it as it can't become serious
    D. realize that it is more serious than any other type of injury

Questions 22-24.

DIRECTIONS: Answer Questions 22 to 24 ONLY according to the information given in the following passage.

GOOD EMPLOYEE PRACTICES

As a City employee, you will be expected to take an interest in your work and perform the duties of your job to the best of your ability and in a spirit of cooperation. Nothing shows an interest in your work more than coming to work on time, not only at the start of the day but also when returning from lunch. If it is necessary for you to keep a personal appointment at lunch hour which might cause a delay in getting back to work on time, you should explain the situation to your supervisor and get his approval to come back a little late before you leave for lunch.

You should do everything that is asked of you willingly and consider important even the small jobs that your supervisor gives you. Although these jobs may seem unimportant, if you forget to do them or if you don't do them right, trouble may develop later.

Getting along well with your fellow workers will add much to the enjoyment of your work. You should respect your fellow workers and try to see their side when a disagreement arises. The better you get along with your fellow workers and your supervisor, the better you will like your job and the better you will be able to do it.

22. According to the above passage, in your job as a City employee, you are expected to 22.___

    A. show a willingness to cooperate on the job
    B. get your supervisor's approval before keeping any personal appointments at lunch hour
    C. avoid doing small jobs that seem unimportant
    D. do the easier jobs at the start of the day and the more difficult ones later on

23. According to the above passage, getting to work on time shows that you 23.___

    A. need the job
    B. have an interest in your work
    C. get along well with your fellow workers
    D. like your supervisor

24. According to the above passage, the one of the following statements that is NOT true is   24.____
    A. if you do a small job wrong, trouble may develop
    B. you should respect your fellow workers
    C. if you disagree with a fellow worker, you should try to see his side of the story
    D. the less you get along with your supervisor, the better you will be able to do your job

Questions 25-35.   VOCABULARY

25. The porter cleaned the VACANT room.   25.____
    In this sentence, the word VACANT means nearly the same as
    A. empty   B. large   C. main   D. crowded

26. The supervisor gave a BRIEF report to his men.   26.____
    In this sentence, the word BRIEF means nearly the same as
    A. long   B. safety   C. complete   D. short

27. The supervisor told him to CONNECT the two pieces.   27.____
    In this sentence, the word CONNECT means nearly the same as
    A. join   B. paint   C. return   D. weigh

28. Standing on the top of a ladder is RISKY.   28.____
    In this sentence, the word RISKY means nearly the same as
    A. dangerous   B. sensible   C. safe   D. foolish

29. He RAISED the cover of the machine.   29.____
    In this sentence, the word RAISED means nearly the same as
    A. broke   B. lifted   C. lost   D. found

30. The form used for reporting the finished work was REVISED.   30.____
    In this sentence, the word REVISED means nearly the same as
    A. printed   B. ordered   C. dropped   D. changed

31. He did his work RAPIDLY.   31.____
    In this sentence, the word RAPIDLY means nearly the same as
    A. carefully   B. quickly   C. slowly   D. quietly

32. The worker was OCCASIONALLY late   32.____
    In this sentence, the word OCCASIONALLY means nearly the same as
    A. sometimes   B. often   C. never   D. always

33. He SELECTED the best tool for the job.   33.____
    In this sentence, the word SELECTED means nearly the same as
    A. bought   B. picked   C. lost   D. broke

34. He needed ASSISTANCE to lift the package.
    In this sentence, the word ASSISTANCE means nearly the same as

    A. strength   B. time   C. help   D. instructions

35. The tools were ISSUED by the supervisor.
    In this sentence, the word ISSUED means nearly the same as

    A. collected
    B. cleaned up
    C. given out
    D. examined

KEY (CORRECT ANSWERS)

1. C
2. B
3. C
4. B
5. A

6. C
7. C
8. D
9. B
10. B

11. C
12. D
13. A
14. A
15. A

16. C
17. D
18. B
19. D
20. C

21. A
22. A
23. B
24. D
25. A

26. D
27. A
28. A
29. B
30. D

31. B
32. A
33. B
34. C
35. C

ARITHMETICAL REASONING
EXAMINATION SECTION
TEST 1

DIRECTIONS: Each question or incomplete statement is followed by several suggested answers or completions. Select the one that BEST answers the question or completes the statement. *PRINT THE LETTER OF THE CORRECT ANSWER IN THE SPACE AT THE RIGHT.*

1. A custodial assistant takes an average of forty minutes to mop 1,000 square feet of floor. The amount of time this custodial assistant should take to mop the floor of a rectangular corridor eight feet wide by sixty feet long is, on the average, MOST NEARLY _____ minutes.   1._____

   A. 10   B. 20   C. 30   D. 40

2. An auditorium eighty feet by 100 feet must be swept in one hour. If each custodial assistant takes fifteen minutes to sweep 1,000 square feet of auditorium area, the number of custodial assistants that must be assigned to complete the sweeping in one hour is   2._____

   A. 1   B. 2   C. 3   D. 4

3. A detergent manufacturer recommends mixing 8 ounces of detergent in one gallon of water to prepare a cleaning solution. The amount of the same detergent which should be mixed with thirty gallons of water to obtain the same strength cleaning solution is _____ ounces.   3._____

   A. 24   B. 30   C. 240   D. 380

4. The floor area of a corridor 8 feet wide and 72 feet long is MOST NEARLY _____ square feet.   4._____

   A. 80   B. 420   C. 580   D. 870

5. A water tank that is 5 feet in diameter and 30 feet high has a volume of MOST NEARLY _____ cubic feet.   5._____

   A. 150   B. 250   C. 600   D. 1,200

6. The circumference of a circle with a radius of 5 inches is MOST NEARLY _____ inches.   6._____

   A. 31.3   B. 30.0   C. 20.1   D. 13.4

7. Suppose that you are the custodian-engineer and an employee works for you at the rate of $8.70 per hour with time and one-half paid for time worked after 40 hours in one week. His gross pay for working 53 hours in one week is MOST NEARLY   7._____

   A. $461.10   B. $482.10   C. $487.65   D. $517.65

8. Suppose that you are the custodian-engineer and one of your employees has gotten gross earnings of $437.10 for the week, all of which is subject to deductions at the rate of 4.8%.
   The amount which should be deducted from the employee's gross earnings for the week is MOST NEARLY

   A. $2.10   B. $14.70   C. $17.70   D. $20.97

9. The directions on the label of a bottle of detergent call for mixing four ounces of detergent with one gallon of water to make a cleaning solution for washing floors. In order to obtain a larger amount of solution of the same strength, one quart of the detergent should be mixed with _____ gallons of water.

   A. 2   B. 4   C. 6   D. 8

10. The area of a lawn which is 58 feet wide by 96 feet long is MOST NEARLY _____ square feet.

    A. 5,000   B. 5,500   C. 6,000   D. 6,500

11. In a building which is heated by an oil-fired boiler, 2,100 gallons of fuel oil were burned in a period in which the degree days reached a total of 1,400.
    If all other conditions remained constant, the number of gallons of fuel oil that would be burned in this building during a period in which the degree days reached a total of 3,600 is

    A. 2,400   B. 2,900   C. 4,800   D. 5,400

12. The instructions for mixing a powdered cleaner in water state, *Mix three ounces of powder in a 14-quart pail three-quarters full of water.* A cleaner asks you how much powdered cleaner he should use in a mop truck containing 28 gallons of water to obtain the same strength solution.
    The CORRECT answer is _____ ounces of powder.

    A. 6   B. 8   C. 24   D. 32

13. A custodian-engineer wishes to order sponges in the most economical manner. Keeping in mind that large sponges can be cut up into many smaller sizes, the one of the following that has the LEAST cost per cubic inch of sponge is

    A. 2" x 4" x 6" sponges @ $.48
    B. 4" x 8" x 12" sponges @ $2.88
    C. 4" x 6" x 36" sponges @ $9.60
    D. 6" x 8" x 32" sponges @ $19.20

14. Two cleaners swept four corridors in 24 minutes. Each corridor measured 12 feet x 176 feet.
    The space swept per man per minute was MOST NEARLY _____ square feet.

    A. 50   B. 90   C. 180   D. 350

15. Kerosene costs 60 cents a quart.
    At that rate, two gallons would cost

    A. $2.40   B. $3.60   C. $4.80   D. $6.00

16. The instructions on a container of cleaning compound states, *Mix one pound of compound in 5 gallons of water.* Using these instructions, the amount of compound which should be added to 15 quarts of water is MOST likely _____ ounces.

    A. 3   B. 8   C. 12   D. 48

    16._____

17. Suppose that you are the custodian-engineer and one of your employees has gross earnings of $582.80 for the week, all of which is subject to Social Security deductions at the rate of 4.8%.
    The amount which should be deducted from the employee's gross earnings for the week is MOST NEARLY

    A. $2.80   B. $19.60   C. $23.60   D. $27.96

    17._____

18. Suppose that you are a custodian-engineer and an employee works for you at the rate of $11.60 per hour with time and one-half paid for time worked after 40 hours in one week. His gross pay for working 53 hours in one week is MOST NEARLY

    A. $614.80   B. $642.80   C. $650.20   D. $690.20

    18._____

19. The volume, in cubic feet, of a cylindrical tank 6 feet in diameter x 35 feet long is MOST NEARLY

    A. 210   B. 990   C. 1,260   D. 3,960

    19._____

20. A room 12 feet wide by 25 feet long has a floor area of _____ square feet.

    A. 37   B. 200   C. 300   D. 400

    20._____

21. How many hours will it take a worker to sweep a floor space of 2,800 square feet if he sweeps at the rate of 800 square feet per hour?

    A. 8   B. 6 1/2   C. 3 1/2   D. 2 1/2

    21._____

22. One gallon of water contains

    A. 2 quarts   B. 4 quarts   C. 2 pints   D. 4 pints

    22._____

23. A standard cleaning solution is prepared by mixing 4 ounces of detergent powder in 2 gallons of water.
    The number of ounces of detergent powder needed for the same strength solution in 5 gallons of water is

    A. 4   B. 6   C. 8   D. 10

    23._____

24. The ceiling of a room which measures 20 feet x 30 feet is to be given two coats of paint. If one gallon of paint will cover 500 square feet, the two coats of paint will require a MINIMUM of _____ gallons.

    A. 1.5   B. 2   C. 2.4   D. 3.2

    24._____

25. The floor area of a room which measures 10 feet long by 10 feet wide is _____ square feet.

    A. 20   B. 40   C. 100   D. 1,000

    25._____

KEY (CORRECT ANSWERS)

1. B
2. B
3. C
4. C
5. C

6. A
7. D
8. D
9. D
10. B

11. D
12. D
13. B
14. C
15. C

16. C
17. D
18. D
19. B
20. C

21. C
22. B
23. D
24. C
25. C

SOLUTIONS TO PROBLEMS

1. (8')(60') = 480 sq.ft. Let x = required time in minutes. Then, $\frac{40}{1000} = \frac{x}{480}$. Solving, x = 19.2 or nearly 20.

2. (80')(100') = 8000 sq.ft. Each custodian can sweep (1000)(4) = 4000 sq.ft. in 1 hour. Then, 8000 ÷ 4000 = 2.

3. (8)(30) = 240 ounces

4. (8')(72') = 576 sq.ft. or nearly 580 sq.ft.

5. Volume = $(\pi)(2.5')^2 (30') \approx$ 589 cu.ft. or nearly 600 cu.ft.

6. Circumference = $(2\pi)(5") \approx$ 31.3 sq.in.

7. ($8.70)(40) + ($13.05)(13) = $517.65

8. ($437.10)(.048) ≈ $20.97

9. 1 quart = 32 oz. Then, 32 ÷ 4 = 8 gallons of water

10. (58')(96') = 5568 sq.ft., which is closest to 5500 sq.ft.

11. Let x = number of gallons. Then, $\frac{2100}{1400} = \frac{x}{3600}$. Solving> x= 5400

12. (.75)(14)(.25) = 2.625 gallons of water. Let x = number of ounces of powder needed. Then, $\frac{3}{2.625} = \frac{x}{28}$. Solving, x = 32

13. For selection B, (4")(8")(12") = 384 cu.in., and the cost per cubic inch = $2.88 ÷ 384 = $.0075. This is lower than selections A ($.01), C ($.011), or D ($.015).

14. Two men sweep (4)(12')(176') = 8448 total sq.ft. in 24 min. = 352 sq.ft. per min. Each man sweeps 176 sq.ft. per min ≈ 180 sq.ft. per min.

15. Two gallons = 8 quarts. Then, ($.60)(8) = $4.80

16. 15 quarts = 3.75 gallons of water. Let x = required number of ounces of compound. Then, $\frac{16}{5} = \frac{x}{3.75}$. Solving, x = 12

17. ($582.80)(.048) ≈ $27.96

18. ($11.60 x 40) + ($17.40)(13) = $690.20

19. Volume = $(\pi)(3')^2 (35') \approx$ 990 cu.ft.

20. (12')(25') = 300 sq.ft.

21. 2800 ÷ 800 = 3 1/2 hours

22. One gallon = 4 quarts

23. Let x = required number of ounces. Then, $\frac{4}{2} = \frac{x}{5}$. Solving, x = 10

24. 2 coats means (2)(20')(30') = 1200 sq.ft. Then, 1200 ÷ 500 = 2.4 gallons

25. (10')(10') = 100 sq.ft.

TEST 2

DIRECTIONS: Each question or incomplete statement is followed by several suggested answers or completions. Select the one that BEST answers the question or completes the statement. *PRINT THE LETTER OF THE CORRECT ANSWER IN THE SPACE AT THE RIGHT.*

1. Assume that a certain elevator starter is at work 8 hours a day, which includes 1 hour for lunch and two 15-minute relief periods. The rest of the workday the starter is performing his duties.
   If the starter works 4 days, the TOTAL amount of time the starter will actually be performing his duties is _____ hours.

   A. 24 B. 26 C. 28 D. 32

2. Assume that a certain bank of 18 elevators operating at full capacity could move 3,240 passengers an hour from the main lobby.
   The number of passengers that one of these elevators could move from the lobby every 15 minutes is, on the average,

   A. 12 B. 22 C. 45 D. 180

3. In a certain agency, the amount of absence due to injury or illness was an average of 6 hours a month for each employee.
   If this agency had 335 employees, the TOTAL number of hours lost in a year due to injury or sickness was

   A. 4,020 B. 20,100 C. 24,120 D. 28,140

4. Assume that in a certain building the elevators must handle 16% of the building population during a peak traffic period.
   If the building population is 2,825, the TOTAL number of people the elevators must handle during a peak traffic period is

   A. 396 B. 424 C. 436 D. 452

5. From his coin bank, a boy took 3 half dollars, 8 quarters, 7 dimes, 6 nickels, and 9 pennies to deposit in his school savings account.
   Express in dollars and cents the TOTAL amount of money he deposited.

   A. $2.82 B. $4.59 C. $6.42 D. $7.52

6. If a roast that requires 1 hour and 40 minutes of roasting time has been in the oven for 55 minutes, how many more minutes of roasting time are required?

   A. 30 B. 36 C. 45 D. 55

7. On the first day of its drive, a school raised $40, which was 33 1/3% of its Red Cross quota.
   How much was the quota?

   A. $120 B. $130 C. $140 D. $150

8. When 0.750 is divided by 0.875, the answer is MOST NEARLY

   A. 0.250 B. 0.312 C. 0.624 D. 0.857

9. The circumference of a 6-inch diameter circle is MOST NEARLY _____ feet.

   A. 1.57   B. 2.1   C. 2.31   D. 4.24

10. An 18" piece of cable that weighs 3 pounds per foot has a total weight of _____ pounds.

    A. 5.5   B. 4.5   C. 3.0   D. 1.5

11. The sum of 0.135, 0.040, 0.812, and 0.961 is

    A. 1.424   B. 1.625   C. 1.843   D. 1.948

12. If an elevator carries a load of 1,600 pounds uniformly distributed on a 4 feet by 5 feet floor, the weight per square foot is _____ pounds.

    A. 98   B. 80   C. 65   D. 40

13. If one cubic inch of lead weighs one-quarter of a pound, the weight of a bar of lead 1" high by 2" wide by 8" long is _____ pounds.

    A. 1.8   B. 2.5   C. 3.1   D. 4

14. Assume that 8 mechanics have been assigned to do a job that must be finished in 5 days. At the end of 3 days, the men have completed only half the job.
    In order to complete the job on time in the remaining 2 days, the MINIMUM number of extra men that should be assigned is

    A. 2   B. 3   C. 4   D. 6

15. An elevator supply manufacturer quotes a list price of $625 less 10 and 5 percent for ten contactors.
    The actual cost for these ten contactors is MOST NEARLY

    A. $562   B. $554   C. $534   D. $522

16. To find the largest number of passengers, including the operator, allowed to ride in an elevator, divide the rated capacity of the elevator by 150.
    According to this rule, what is the LARGEST number of passengers NOT counting the operator that may be carried in an elevator with a rated capacity of 3,000 lbs.?

    A. 18   B. 19   C. 20   D. 21

17. Suppose that the work schedule for operators is 5 days a week, 8 hours a day.
    In a period of 4 weeks, with no holidays, how many hours will you be required to be on duty?

    A. 160   B. 180   C. 200   D. 225

18. Mr. Jones takes $200 to cover his expenses for a week. He spends $6.00 for carfare coming to work and $6.00 for carfare going home. He buys a $1 newspaper each day and spends $16.00 for lunch and $5.00 for cigarettes each day.
    How much money does he have left at the end of a 5-day work week?

    A. $30.00   B. $55.00   C. $100.00   D. $170.00

19. Twelve hundred employees work in an office building. 19.____
Twenty percent of these employees work on the 4th floor and 25% work on the 5th floor.
The TOTAL number of employees who work on the 4th and 5th floors together is

   A. 240   B. 300   C. 540   D. 660

20. An elevator makes one roundtrip every 5 minutes, on the average. 20.____
How many roundtrips does it make between 8:15 A.M. and 9:45 A.M.?

   A. 12   B. 18   C. 20   D. 22

21. The floor of an elevator car measures 7 feet by 8 feet 6 inches. 21.____
How many square feet of linoleum would be needed to cover this floor?

   A. 31   B. 42   C. 59 1/2   D. 62 1/2

Questions 22-25.

   DIRECTIONS: Each question consists of a statement. You are to indicate whether the statement is TRUE (T) or FALSE (F).

22. In a city building, there are 20 elevators. If on one day five percent of the elevators are out of order, the number of elevators out of order is 2. 22.____

23. An elevator operator puts in 32 hours of overtime in January, 26 hours in February, 10 hours in March, 10 hours in April, and 27 hours in May. The average amount of overtime this operator worked per month for these five months is 21 hours. 23.____

24. A large city building normally has 45 elevator operators on its day shift. The vacation rules require that only 1/5 be allowed away at any time. The number of operators that may be on vacation at one time is nine. 24.____

25. In a six-story city building, there are 13 offices on the first floor, 19 offices on the second floor, 18 offices on the third floor, 17 offices on the fourth floor, 21 offices on the fifth floor, and 23 offices on the sixth floor. The total number of offices in this building is 109. 25.____

4 (#2)

KEY (CORRECT ANSWERS)

1.	B	11.	D
2.	C	12.	B
3.	C	13.	D
4.	D	14.	C
5.	B	15.	C
6.	C	16.	B
7.	A	17.	A
8.	D	18.	A
9.	A	19.	C
10.	B	20.	B

21. C
22. F
23. T
24. T
25. F

SOLUTIONS TO PROBLEMS

1. 4(8-1-.5) = 26 hours

2. Each elevator can move 3240 ÷ 18 = 180 passengers per hour, which = 45 passengers per 15 minutes.

3. (335)(6)(12) = 24,120 hours per year.

4. (2825)(.16) = 452

5. (3)(.50) + (8)(.25) + (7)(.10) + (6)(.05) + (9)(.01) = $4.59

6. 1 hr. 40 min. - 55 min. = 100 min. - 55 min. = 45 min.

7. $40 ÷ $33\frac{1}{3}$% = $40 ÷ $\frac{1}{3}$ = $120

8. .750 ÷ .875 ≈ .857

9. Circumference = ($\frac{1}{2}$')(π) ≈ 1.57'

10. 18" ÷ 12" = 1.5. Then, (1.5)(3) = 4.5 lbs.

11. .135 + .040 + .812 + .961 = 1.948

12. (4')(5') = 20 sq.ft. Then, 1600 ÷ 20 = 80 lbs. per sq.ft.

13. (1")(2")(8") = 16 cu.in. Then, (16)(1/4) = 4 pounds

14. 8 men x 3 cars = 50% of work; 24 man-days = 50% of work; 48 man-days = 100%; 24 man-days ÷ 2 days = 12 men per day = 4 extra men

15. ($625)(.90)(.95) ≈ $534

16. 3000 ÷ 150 = 20 people, including the operator. Thus, only 19 passengers are allowed.

17. (8)(5)(4) = 160 hours

18. $200 - 5($6.00+$6.00+$1+$16.00+$5.00) = $30.00

19. (1200)(20%+25%) = (1200)(.45) = 540

20. 9:45 AM - 8:15 AM = 90 min. Then, 90 ÷ 5 = 18 roundtrips

21. (7')(8 1/2') = 59 1/2 sq.ft.

22. False; (20)(.05) = 1, not 2.

23. True. (32+26+10+10+27) ÷ 5 = 21

24. True. (45)(1/5) = 9

25. False. 13 + 19 + 18 + 17 + 21 + 23 = 111, not 109

TEST 3

DIRECTIONS: Each question or incomplete statement is followed by several suggested answers or completions. Select the one that BEST answers the question or completes the statement. *PRINT THE LETTER OF THE CORRECT ANSWER IN THE SPACE AT THE RIGHT.*

1. When 60,987 is added to 27,835, the answer is   1._____
   A. 80,712   B. 80,822   C. 87,712   D. 88,822

2. The sum of 693 + 787 + 946 + 355 + 731 is   2._____
   A. 3,512   B. 3,502   C. 3,412   D. 3,402

3. When 2,586 is subtracted from 3,003, the answer is   3._____
   A. 417   B. 527   C. 1,417   D. 1,527

4. When 1.32 is subtracted from 52.6, the answer is   4._____
   A. 3.94   B. 5.128   C. 39.4   D. 51.28

5. When 56 is multiplied by 438, the answer is   5._____
   A. 840   B. 4,818   C. 24,528   D. 48,180

6. When 8.7 is multiplied by .34, the answer is MOST NEARLY   6._____
   A. 2.9   B. 3.0   C. 29.5   D. 29.6

7. When 1/2 is divided by 2/3, the answer is   7._____
   A. 1/3   B. 3/4   C. 1 1/3   D. 3

8. When 8,340 is divided by 38, the answer is MOST NEARLY   8._____
   A. 210   B. 218   C. 219   D. 220

9. Assume that a helper earns $11.16 an hour and that he works 250 seven-hour days a year.   9._____
   His gross yearly salary will be
   A. $19,430   B. $19,530   C. $19,650   D. $19,780

10. On a certain map, a distance of 10 miles is represented by 1/2 inch.   10._____
    If two towns are 3 1/2 inches apart on this map, express, in miles, the actual distance between the two towns.
    A. 70   B. 80   C. 90   D. 100

11. The area of the triangle shown at the right is _____ square inches.   11._____
    A. 120
    B. 240
    C. 360
    D. 480

(triangle with legs 24" and 10", 90° angle)

12. The sum of 1/3 + 2/5 + 5/6 is

    A. 1 17/30   B. 1 3/5   C. 1 5/8   D. 1 5/6

13. The sum of the following dimensions, 3'2 1/4", 0'8 7/8", 2'6 3/8", 2'9 3/4", and 1'0", is

    A. 9'2 7/8"   B. 10'3 1/4"
    C. 10'7 3/7"   D. 11'4 1/4"

14. If the scale of a drawing is 1/8" to the foot, then a 1/2" measurement on the drawing would represent an actual length of _____ feet.

    A. 2   B. 4   C. 8   D. 16

15. Assume that an area measures 78 feet by 96 feet.
    The number of square feet in this area is

    A. 7,478   B. 7,488   C. 7,498   D. 7,508

16. If a can of paint costs $17.50, four dozen cans of this paint will cost

    A. $837.50   B. $840.00   C. $842.50   D. $845.00

17. The number of square feet in 1 square yard is

    A. 3   B. 6   C. 9   D. 12

18. The sum of 4 1/2 inches, 3 1/4 inches, and 7 1/2 inches is 1 foot _____ inches.

    A. 3   B. 3 1/4   C. 3 1/2   D. 4

19. If a room is 10 feet by 18 feet, the number of square feet of floor space in it is

    A. 1,800   B. 180   C. 90   D. 28

20. A jacket that was marked at $12.50 was sold for $10.
    What was the rate of discount on the marked price?

    A. 10%   B. 15%   C. 18%   D. 20%

Questions 21-25.

DIRECTIONS: Each question consists of a statement. You are to indicate whether the statement is TRUE (T) or FALSE (F).

21. Three-eighths (3/8") of an inch is equivalent to .0375".

22. A floor measuring 12 feet by 9 feet contains 36 sq.ft.

23. A box measuring 18 inches square and 16 inches deep will have a volume of 36 cubic feet.

24. If the charge for a long distance telephone call is 50¢ for the first 5 minutes and 7? for each minute after that, then for 85¢ a person could speak for 10 minutes.

25. If 15 gallons of gasoline cost $14.85 and you use up 10 gallons, then the value of the gasoline which is still left is $4.95.

KEY (CORRECT ANSWERS)

1. D	11. A
2. A	12. A
3. A	13. B
4. D	14. B
5. C	15. B
6. B	16. B
7. B	17. C
8. C	18. B
9. B	19. B
10. A	20. D

21. F
22. F
23. F
24. T
25. T

SOLUTIONS TO PROBLEMS

1. 60,987 + 27,835 = 88,822

2. 693 + 787 + 946 + 355 + 731 = 3512

3. 3003 - 2586 = 417

4. 52.6 - 1.32 = 51.28

5. (56)(438) = 24,528

6. (8.7)(.34) = 2.958 ≈ 3.0

7. $\frac{1}{2} \div \frac{2}{3} = \frac{1}{2} \cdot \frac{3}{2} = \frac{3}{4}$

8. 8340 ÷ 38 ≈ 219.47 ≈ 219

9. ($11.16)(7)(250) = $19,530

10. 3 1/2" ÷ 1/2" = 7. Then, (7)(10) = 70 miles

11. Area = (1/2)(10")(24") = 120 sq.in.

12. $\frac{1}{3} + \frac{2}{5} + \frac{5}{6} = \frac{10}{30} + \frac{12}{30} + \frac{25}{30} = \frac{47}{30} = 1\frac{17}{30}$

13. 3'2 1/4" + 0'8 7/8" + 2'6 3/8" + 2'9 3/4" + 1'0" = 8'25 18/8" = 10'3 1/4"

14. 1/2" ÷ 1/8" = 4. Then, (4)(1 ft.) = 4 ft.

15. (78')(96') = 7488 sq.ft.

16. (48)($17.50) = $840.00

17. 1 sq.yd. = (3)(3) = 9 sq.ft.

18. 4 1/2" + 3 1/4" + 7 1/2" = 14 5/4" = 1 foot 3 1/4 inches

19. (10')(18') = 180 sq.ft.

20. $12.50 - $10 = $2.50. Then, $2.50 ÷ $12.50 = .20 = 20%

21. False. 3/8" = .375", not .0375"

22. False. (12')(9') = 108 sq.ft., not 36 sq.ft.

23. False. (18")(18")(16") = 5184 cu.in. = 3 cu.ft., not 36 cu.ft.
    Note: 1 cu.ft. = 1728 cu.in.

24. True. The cost for 10 minutes = .50 + (.07)(10-5) = .85

25. True. $14.85 ÷ 15 = $.99 per gallon. The value of 5 gallons = (5)($.99) = $4.95

BASIC FUNDAMENTALS OF THE MAINTENANCE OF FLOORS

CONTENTS

	Page
FLOOR TYPES	1
BUFFING TECHNIQUE	11
STRIPPING	13
FINISHING FLOORS	18
SPRAY BUFFING	20
CARPET CARE	22

BASIC FUNDAMENTALS OF THE MAINTENANCE OF FLOORS

FLOOR TYPES

I. Resilient—Elastic or Soft Floor

A. ASPHALT TILE

1. Made from asphalt-treated asbestos fibers, with an inert filler (usually limestone) to give it hardness. For darker colored tile, gilsonite (black) asphalt is used. In lighter colors, coal tar resins are used for binders. Ingredients are mixed under heat and transferred to hot rollers, where the mix is rolled into uniform thickness.

2. Precautions. Never use varnish, spirit waxes or solvent-type cleaners. Do not sweep asphalt tile floors with sweeping compounds containing fine oil or petroleum distillities.

B. VINYL TILE

1. Vinyl plastic (resin) is manufactured with vinyl-resin along with color pigments and fillers. It has all the advantages of asphalt tile, plus being more flexible, and almost impervious and immune to damage by petroleum products.

C. RUBBER TILE

1. Is generally made from synthetic, reclaimed, or pure rubber; color pigments; and inert fillers. The mix is fused and used like other rubber products, molded under pressure to required thickness, and then made into sheets of tile. It has the advantages of asphalt and vinyl floors, plus being the most pliable. It recovers from indention and resists cracking.

2. Precautions. Oil, grease, naphtha and similar petroleum products will soften and deteriorate rubber tile. Do not sweep with sweeping compounds containing oils or petroleum distillities. Air and sunlight cause rubber tile to crack or check. Do not use shellac, varnish, lacquer, alkaline soaps, or abrasives on rubber floors.

D. LINOLEUM

1. It is made of oxidized linseed oil, resins, and other filler material thoroughly mixed with ground cork and color pigments. The mixture is pressed out on a backing material (normally burlap) by running the mix through rollers, then curing at high temperature.

2. Precautions. Same as asphalt tile.

E. MASTIC FLOORS

1. Similar to asphalt tile in composition, but ingredients are heated on the job and troweled on, to form a seamless flooring material.

2. Precautions. Same as asphalt tile.

F. CORK FLOORING

1. Is made by compressing or baking cork curlings and ground cork, or by adding synthetic resin binders. The baking causes natural gums and resins in the cork to liquify, thus binding together the cork particles.

GENERAL POINTS TO BE OBSERVED IN MAINTENANCE OF ALL RESILIENT FLOORING:

1. All resilient flooring material should be cleaned and a floor finish applied (either wax or

synthetic) as soon as floor has been allowed to set up. These floors should be cleaned and a finish applied on regular schedule, throughout the life of the floor.

2. Being a semi-soft material, it should be kept free of sand and dirt, which may scratch or discolor the surface.

3. Thorough dusting with a properly treated dust mop is important. To reduce the number of scrubbings necessary, oil and solvent type dust mop treatment should not be used. Damp or wet mopping should be utilized to remove surface soil conditions (mud, water and sand).

4. Spray buffing in heavy traffic areas will maintain these areas looking as well as non-traffic areas. It lengthens the time between stripping. Remember that spray buffing is not a cure for all maintenance problems.

5. Buffing is an absolute necessity in areas where traffic is heavy.

6. The legs of chairs, tables, and desks should be equipped with coasters or glides to prevent denting or marking of floor.

II. Hard Floors

A. CONCRETE

1. Concrete floors are mixtures of cement with varying proportions of sand and gravel. The porosity and smoothness of the surface depends upon the mix and the hardening and finishing process. Color pigments are often added to the topping mix when concrete is used as a decorative floor material.

2. Maintenance for Concrete Floors:

a. Concrete floors protected by concrete sealer and wax will require only dust mopping or floor brushing to keep them clean and attractive. Concrete floors may be cleaned with any mild cleaning solution; however, care should be taken in proper rinsing.

b. If a concrete floor dusts excessively, it should be scrubbed with a neutral soap and sealed. Proper sealing will greatly lengthen concrete floor life, prevent dusting, and make maintenance easier and more economical. When traffic lanes begin to show, the floor can easily be touched up. Properly done, this treatment will not show an overlap.

c. Concrete floors can be waxed rather than sealed. However, better results will be achieved by sealing the floor and then applying a coat of wax. After this treatment, periodic buffing, using a fine nylon disc, will greatly reduce maintenance time, and decrease the frequency of stripping and refinishing.

B. TERRAZZO

1. Terrazzo is one of the oldest flooring materials. It was used in pre-Christian times in many palaces and mansions of ancient rulers and merchants.

2. It is a hard, durable composition material, made up of marble chips and cement matrix. This surface, after hardening for a time, is wet ground under pressure with stone grinders. Because of its pattern, terrazzo does not readily show soil and stays presentable longer than floors of one color.

3. Special Precautions in Maintenance of Terrazzo:

MAINTENANCE OF FLOORS

a. Cleaning materials containing acids or alkalines should be avoided, since the acid or alkali eats into the cement and loosens the marble chips.

b. Avoid abrasive powder cleaners because they encourage "dusting." This type of cleaner actually wears away the floor, and its ill effects are noticeable within a short period of time.

c. Cleaning crystals of a phosphate nature should never be used. A residue remains after the water has evaporated and acts in much the same way as water when it is allowed to stand in a concrete formation and is then frozen. In other words, the crystals fill up porous spots in the cement; and as they dry, they expand. The expansion loosens the marble chips; this is called "spalling."

d. Avoid sweeping compounds containing oil. These will penetrate and discolor terrazzo.

4. Maintenance for Terrazzo Floors

a. In scrubbing a terrazzo floor, do not use steel wool. It is best to use a brush for scrubbing because the steel wool is softer than the terrazzo and may become abraded. Bits of the wool left on the floor will rust and stain the terrazzo. Also, the use of steel wool on terrazzo can result in black carbon marks. Clean terrazzo with neutral, synthetic, free-rinsing liquid detergent. These detergents will leave no unsightly residue that often necessitates special work and materials to remove it.

b. Terrazzo floors should be mopped frequently and rinsed thoroughly. Dirty water will stain if left too long; it leaves a gummy hardened accumulation of film which is not easily removed.

c. The use of a solvent type "water white" sealer on terrazzo will prevent dusting and spalling. However, a heavy surface film of this material allowed to build up will result in severe traffic laning. Color variations in the floor may also appear.

d. Properly applied, colorless, buffable-type terrazzo seal, well-rubbed out, tends to harden the surface, helps hold the marble chips together, and virtually stops penetration of water, stains, oils, gums and other damaging materials. The finish will have a satin-like sheen.

e. Either solvent or water emulsion-type wax can be used on terrazzo. However, only waxes manufacured from light colored products should be used. Solvent-type wax manufactured from waxed having a very dark color, or solvent waxes to which artificial coloring matter has been added, would definitely cause a discoloration of terrazzo. Serious discoloration could also occur if a water wax emulsion made from dark colored waxes is applied to a terrazzo floor.

C. MARBLE

1. Marble is a natural product of crystallized rock, composed of carbonate of lime. Generally, marble used in the interior of buildings for decorative purposes is of the polished, finished type which reflects light because of its glossy surface. This also emphasizes color and marking. Marble used for interior floors may have a "honed" or a "sand" finish.

a. Travertine marble, recognized by its small pits and tarnish-colored surface, requires only cleaning, as does polished marble. Travertine is used generally as wainscot or other trim material.

2. On all types of marble, except the Travertine, sealing is recommended. The primary purpose of this treatment is to provide maximum protection to the marble itself, which is very soft and porous. Ordinary dirt and grease are sealed out of the floor, and because the pits and voids have been filled, the soil is held on the surface and is easy to remove through usual maintenance methods.

3. Marble floors sealed and finished with a good, colorless, buffable type terrazzo sealer can be maintained dry with only occasional mopping. Sealers of solvent cut resin or lacquer nature, used on marble floors, result in traffic laning, uneven appearance of the floor surface, and over a period of time, discoloration of the surface.

4. Special Precautions in Maintenance of Marble:

a. Never use an acid cleaner. It will destroy polish and eventually burn. The end result will be discoloration and disintegration of the marble.

b. Do not use scouring bricks or harsh abrasives. These materials will destroy polish and mar the surface.

c. Bar, powder, or liquid soaps should not be used on marble surfaces. They may form insoluble deposits which accumulate on the surface. This discoloration cannot be readily removed and will become a slip hazard when wet.

d. Never use oily sweeping compounds on marble surfaces. Their use will evenutally discolor the floor.

e. Quick action "lightening" cleaners are apt to be acid in action. The life and finish of the marble will be sacrificed for immediate results.

5. Maintenance for Marble Floors:

a. The secret to beautiful marble is merely keeping it clean after the original sealing treatment. Complicated cleaning agents and procedures will rarely be needed if the marble surfaces are maintained properly and regularly. When complete cleaning is necessary, use a neutral, free-rinsing detergent that will not leave a slippery or unattractive residue.

b. Marble spalling and deterioration can be caused through neglect. Marble is not indestructable, and when neglected, the accumulated dirt and grease can completely deteriorate and damage the surface beyond repair.

D. OXYCHLORIDE

1. Oxychloride, sometimes called magnasite, is similar to concrete. It is produced in many colors. It can be installed with two types of finish. One type of finish is trowelled on. The other type of finish is ground and gives the appearance of being terrazzo. It can be laid over nearly any type of sub-floor and produces a surface which is rather resilient, yet dense and strong. However, magnasite is a somewhat porous and soft material as compared to terrazzo or concrete.

2. Special Precautions in Maintenance of Oxychloride:

a. Avoid use of strong alkalies for cleaning.

b. Acids used in some cleaning materials tend to dissolve oxychloride due to chemical reaction and should not be used.

MAINTENANCE OF FLOORS

c. Avoid excessive use of water. This material is ever-thirsty, and deterioration of the binder will result.

3. Maintenance for Oxychloride Floors:

a. In cleaning, a neutral soap or a non-alkaline detergent should be used. The application procedure is listed under asphalt tile.

b. Oxychloride flooring is porous and may be sealed with a penetrating-type sealer. Sealing will fill the pores of the floor covering, and maintenance work will become easier.

c. When excessively soiled, oxychloride floors should be scrubbed with a floor machine, using a scrubbing brush. However, the excessive use of water will damage some of the fillers, and will also attack the magnesium oxychloride binder and deteriorate it. For this reason, oxychloride floors should be sealed and waxed.

d. Solvent-type wax should be used on this flooring. Oily floor dressings should not be used as they could result in serious discoloration. Sweeping compounds containing organic dyes and free oil could also cause discoloration, and any sand present in the compound could result in the scratching and abrading of the rather soft oxychloride floor.

E. HARD TILE

1. Ceramic tile or "hard tile" is made of finely ground clay and baked to the hardness of stone. The various types include ceramic mosaic, quarry, and clear glaze.

2. Hard tile is naturally durable and resistant to soil defacement; but to get full value from a large investment, it has to have the same care as more susceptible flooring materials. Hard tile can be either glazed or unglazed. Tile used as flooring material is usually unglazed. Glazed tile is normally used as wall surfacings.

3. Special Precautions in Maintenance of Hard Tile:

a. Avoid solutions of strong alkaline cleaners, such as tri-sodium phosphate and sal soda. These cleaners penetrate the cement grout between the tile and upon drying, leave crystallized deposits. Continued use of alkaline cleaners will cause the crystallized deposits to accumulate and swell, causing disintegration of the grout.

b. Do not use steel wool for cleaning hard tile. The tile is harder than the steel wool and will abrade the wool, causing discoloration of the tile. Abrasive cleansers should never be used on the glazed surfaces.

c. Do not use acid cleaners, not because they will injure the tile, but because they will tend to destroy the cement grout. They may also dull glazed or ceramic tile.

d. Oily dust mops and sweeping compounds should not be used for maintenance of hard tile floors.

4. Maintenance for Hard Tile Floors:

a. About the only maintenance process for glazed tile floors consists of dusting and spot washing. Non-alkaline synthetic cleaners are recommended for cleaning.

b. Tile used as a flooring material resists most traffic stains, but it can suffer from the erosive action of abrasion. This means not only the wear and tear from traffic; but also from abrasive cleansers, which in time, will scratch or dull the finish.

c. A penetrating sealer, such as the type used for terrazzo, will prove to be a protection for the surface and will also protect cement grout from undue deterioration. Surface sealers which leave a heavy film of a non-buffable nature should not be used.

d. Waxing a hard tile floor is not recommended because wax may become a safety hazard. Where safety is not a factor, either the water emulsion or solvent wax can be used.

F. WOOD

1. The use of hard wood floors is as old as civilization. Their durability has been an important factor in their wide use. Wood floors, properly maintained, are capable of retaining their natural good looks for a long period of time. Wood can last a lifetime and longer.

2. Special Precautions in Maintenance of Wood:

a. Use a minimum amount of water to maintain wood floors. Excessive water may enter through the ends of the wood and cause swelling or warping.

b. When wood floors are set in mastic, exercise extreme care in the use of sealers, spirit waxes, solvent cleaners, and water.

c. Select and use a maintenance method which eliminates or minimizes the necessity for resanding.

3. Maintenance for Wood Floors:

a. Any good soap, except those strongly alkaline, can be used for cleaning wood floors. However, scrubbing, or even wet mopping will ultimately damage a wood floor.

b. It is most important to understand the adverse effects of water, oil, and alkali soaps on wood. Water raises the grain on wood floors, causes swelling and warping, and in general, creates a rough surface that is difficult to maintain. Where wood floors are bonded to a sub-floor, penetrating water will weaken the bond and cause loosening. In addition, water discolors wood, gives it a musty odor, and causes it to rot. Oil softens wood, darkens it, and creates a sticky surface that picks up and holds dirt. Alkali cleaners can stain and darken wood floors.

c. Wood floors of any type require positive sealing. Seals, manufactured specifically for wood floor application, protect against penetration of moisture, and properly formulated, are resistant to acids, alkalies, and oils.

d. The two general classifications of wood sealers are called surface seal and penetrating seal. The type used depends upon the floor usage.

e. Surface sealers are used for floors which are not subjected to heavy traffic. This type forms a perceptible film on top of the wood while penetrating it to a certain extent, and sealing. The surface seals are preferred for the sake of appearance.

f. The true penetrating sealers protect the wood surface by filling the pores but leave little actual surface. The penetrating seal is better for areas of heavy traffic since its "stain" finish is less subject to marking.

g. Traffic lanes, which show up in time, can be resealed without treating the entire area. The worn areas need only be scrubbed and given a light coating. If sufficient care is used in doing the patching, the former worn spots will not be noticeable.

MAINTENANCE OF FLOORS

h. Waxing, after the seal application, is an ideal treatment to provide maximum appearance and protection. Use of a solvent-type wax is highly recommended. It will prolong the life of the wood surface by reducing the need for mopping.

STAIN REMOVAL FOR RESILIENT FLOORS

A properly maintained resilient floor covering should have sufficient wax or floor finish on the surface to protect it against most water based stains, and many oil- and solvent-based stains. Freshly spilled stains should be wiped up or blotted immediately before they have a chance to dry. Dried stains, being more difficult to remove and usually of questionable origin, may require more than one treatment of different stain removers. Never use a solvent-type cleaner (turpentine, naphtha, dry-cleaning solution) on asphalt or rubber.

GENERAL POINTS TO OBSERVE:

1. Act promptly in treating stains or spots. Stains or spots are most easily removed when fresh. Use the mildest treatment, first. Maybe blotting paper or cold water sponging will remove the stain.

2. Before treatment of the stain, wet the area around it with clear water. This tends to stop the spread of the cleaner. Always work from the outside toward the center to prevent leaving a cleaning ring.

3. Several applications may be necessary before the stain can be completely removed.

4. Water is considered a good solvent. When possible its use is recommended first. In any case, it is always best to use the simplest procedure.

5. It is important to know the surface to be treated and the nature of the stain before trying to remove the stain. If you do not know, leave it alone. Call in an expert.

   a. Is the stain water-borne? If so, water will remove it.

   b. Is the stain alcohol-borne (for example, iodine)? If so, alcohol will remove it.

   c. Is the stain alkali? Then use an acid to neutralize it.

   d. Is the stain acid? If so, use alkali.

MAINTENANCE OF FLOORS

TYPE OF STAIN	TREATMENT
Acids	Clean with diluted general purpose cleaner. Strong acids may require neutralization with ammonia solution.
Adhesives, Flooring	Rub with nylon pad dipped in dilute cleaner. Some mastic adhesives may respond better to concentrated cleaner and nylon pad. Use alcohol on asphalt or rubber.
Alcoholic Beverages	Rub with nylon pad dipped in dilute cleaner. Wine stains might require alcohol or hydrogen peroxide.
Alkalies	Neutralize with acetic acid 5% solution (vinegar), rinse thoroughly, dry and apply polish.
Blood	First, the soiled area should be washed with plain, clear, cold water. Then, a few drops of ammonia should be applied to the area.
Candle Wax	Scrape off with putty knife. Wash with dilute cleaner, rinse, dry and apply polish. Use concentrated cleaner for asphalt and rubber.
Candy	Scrape off with putty knife. Apply diluted cleaner, rub with nylon pad.
Chewing Gum	Scrape off with putty knife. Scraping may be more effective if gum is first frozen with dry ice. Wash with diluted cleaner, rinse, dry and apply polish. Use concentrated cleaner for asphalt and rubber.
Chocolate	Scrape off with putty knife. Rub with nylon pad dipped in dilute cleaner. Rinse, dry and apply polish if necessary.
Cigarette Burns	Rub with coarse, then mild, nylon pad dipped in dilute cleaner. Rinse and dry. Slight indentations may require patching.

MAINTENANCE OF FLOORS

Coffee	Wash with diluted cleaner. A build-up of residue may require the use of mild nylon pad. If stain is old, place over it an absorbent cloth saturated with a glycerin solution. Let stand for about a half hour. Then, reclean with dilute cleaner. A deep stain may require the use of hydrogen peroxide.
Crayon	Scrape off with putty knife. Rub residual mark with nylon pad dipped in solution. Wash with dilute cleaner, rinse, dry and apply polish if necessary. Use concentrated cleaner for asphalt and rubber.
Fruit Juices	Use dilute cleaner. Persistent stains may require hydrogen peroxide.
Grass Stains	See Coffee
Ink, Ball Point	Clean with naphtha and/or alcohol (for asphalt and rubber, rub with nylon pad dipped in concentrated cleaner). Rinse, dry and spot polish.
Ink, Washable	Use diluted cleaner. If ink is soaked into floor, apply an alcohol-soaked blotter for several minutes. Wash with dilute cleaner, rinse, dry and apply polish.
Iodine	Clean with alcohol or an ammonia-saturated cloth. Deep stains may require longer contact with ammonia-saturated cotton. Rinse with dilute cleaner, clear water, dry and apply polish.
Lipstick	Scrape with putty knife. Rub residual stain with nylon pad dipped in concentrated cleaner. Deep stains may require the use of hydrogen peroxide followed by dilute cleaner. Rinse, dry and apply polish if necessary.
Nail Polish	Clean with acetone (use alcohol and nylon pad on asphalt and rubber).
Oil and Grease	Use diluted cleaner, rinse and dry.

	For Persistent Stains
	Cover stain with cotton batting soaked in hydrogen peroxide. On top of this, lay cotton batting soaked in ammonia. Repeat treatment as necessary until stain is removed.
Paint	Use paint remover sparingly. (Do not use solvent on asphalt and rubber. Rub with nylon pad.) Apply diluted cleaner, rinse, dry and polish.
Black Rubber Marks	Rub with nylon stripping pad dipped in concentrated cleaner. Apply dilute cleaner, rinse, dry and polish. For wood or other non-resilient floors, rub with pad dipped in cleaner or naphtha.
Rust	Use oxalic acid solution, rinse thoroughly, dry and apply polish if necessary.
Shellac	Clean with alcohol. Apply diluted cleaner, rinse, dry and polish.
Shoe Polish	Rub with nylon pad dipped in concentrated cleaner. Apply dilute cleaner, rinse, dry and polish.
Solvents	Solvents may roughen floor or cause color mixing. Burnish with an abrasive pad or nylon pad. Apply floor polish.
Tar	See Chewing Gum.
Tobacco	Apply diluted cleaner. On porous floors use lemon juice and water or equal parts of alcohol and glycerin. It may be necessary to bleach the stain with hydrogen peroxide or a liquid bleach.
Urine	Apply diluted cleaning solution. If stain is old, use oxalic acid solution followed by cleaner. Rinse, dry and polish if necessary.

MAINTENANCE OF FLOORS

BUFFING TECHNIQUE

PURPOSE: To remove surface soil and renew the protective surface coating.

EQUIPMENT:

    Electric floor machine
    Nylon pads
    Treated cloths
    Brush or Drive assembly
    Sweeping tool, or
    Broom and broom bags

SAFETY PRECAUTIONS:

1. Do not leave machine unattended and plugged in.

2. Handle the machine carefully. Keep both hands on machine.

3. Always remove all cord off hooks and handle before beginning the buffing operation.

4. Check cord and plug for breaks and loose connections.

PROCEDURE

1. Assemble equipment. Take to assigned area.

2. Dust/sweep floors.

3. Tilt machine back on wheels and handle.

4. Straddle handle. Secure brush or drive assembly to drum of machine. Turn counterclockwise to lock.

5. Plug machine into most convenient outlet.

6. Stand machine on brush.

7. Adjust handle to proper height for comfort and ease of handling.

8. Raise wheels.

PROCEDURE

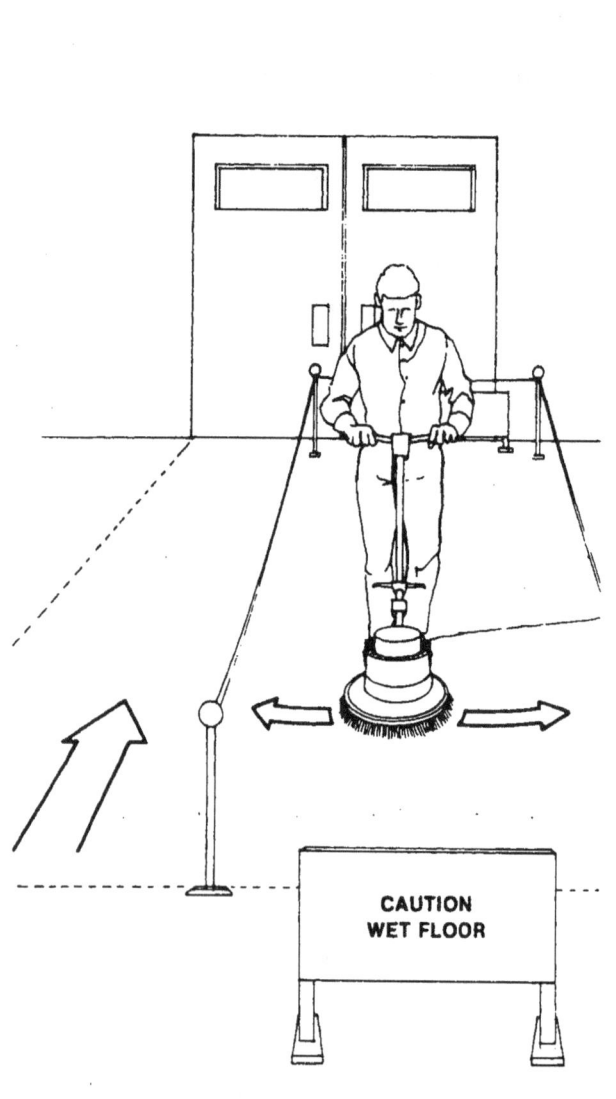

9. Begin buffing:
    a. Place cord over shoulder to keep out of path of machine. Start machine directly in front of the operator.

    b. Press downward on handle to move machine to right.

    c. Raise the handle to move the machine to the left.

    d. Move machine slowly in a left to right and right to left, or side to side arc pattern.

    e. Walk backward which facilitates easier movement of machine. However, it is safer to move forward.

10. Continue this procedure until area is completed.

11. Take equipment to utility room. Remove brush or drive assembly and pads, and wash. Wipe machine and cord off. Return to designated area.

MAINTENANCE OF FLOORS

STRIPPING
(Wet and Dry)

PURPOSE: To remove finish and embedded dirt, and to prepare floor for refinishing. This operation is performed by a combination of chemical action of the cleaning agent and the action of the brush or pad attached to an electric floor machine.

EQUIPMENT:

- Utility cart
- Nylon stripping pads
- Buckets and wringers on dolly (two)
- Mopheads and handles (two)
- Putty knife (long handle)
- Vacuum cleaner (wet and dry)
- Cloths
- Wet floor signs
- Sweeping tool—treated cloths, or Broom—broom bags
- Coving brush and handle
- Electric floor machine and attachments
- Drive assembly
- Scrubbing brush with pad holder
- Stripping agent
- Gloves
- Dustpan and Counter brush

SAFETY PRECAUTIONS:

1. Strip floor only on the advice of the supervisor.

2. Always sweep (use sweeping tool or covered broom) or vacuum before stripping.

3. Post area with wet floor signs.

4. Strip a small section (approximately six feet) at a time to avoid standing in solution.

5. Do not use an extension cord that is smaller than cord on machine.

6. Make sure that electric cord is free of any breaks and that the plug and outlets are grounded. Do not remove grounding prong.

7. Authorities state that adapters should not be used on portable electrical commercial equipment.

8. Place electric cord over shoulder to prevent it from becoming entangled in the machine. Hold a loop of the cord in hand so that a sudden motion will not jerk the cord and break wires.

PROCEDURE

Wet

1. Assemble equipment. Prepare solution. Take to designated area.

2. Put area out of order. Post wet floor signs.

3. Move furniture and disconnect all electrical appliances and equipment.

4. Vacuum or dust area with sweeping tool or covered broom. Remove debris with dustpan and counter brush.

PROCEDURE

5. Scrub baseboards. Use coving brush, baseboard cleaning attachment, or improvised nylon pad on mop handle to remove built-up soil from baseboards in areas where applicable.

6. Apply stripping solution to floor surface with mop. Allow to stand for two to three minutes.

7. Begin scrubbing far enough from walls to prevent the splashing of soil and solution.

8. Carry solution on floor with motion of the machine. Move slowly, but continuously—using a side-to-side, overlapping, arc pattern. Cover a six-foot path. If floors are pitted or dented, scrub in a criss-cross pattern. Turn machine slightly on edge, either to the right or left, (heeling) to remove "hard to remove" marks.

9. Pick up soil and solution. Use mop or wet vacuum. In extremely soiled areas, it may be necessary to repeat the above procedures.

10. Rinse floor and baseboards. Apply enough rinse water to completely remove all soil and solution.

11. Pick up rinse water with mop or wet vacuum.

12. Re-rinse floor surface with clear water several times in order to free surface of detergent. This is important because detergent harms some types of floor surfacing.

13. Continue entire procedure until area is completed.

14. Take equipment to utility room. Wash and dry. Wash off machines, cords, brushes, and pads. Return all equipment to designated stor-

MAINTENANCE OF FLOORS — 15

PROCEDURE

---

age area. Restock utility cart. Place mopheads in plastic liner/bag and place in laundry bag; then store in designated area to be picked up and laundered.

- - - - - - - - - - - - - - -

Dry

This procedure at Saint Elizabeths Hospital is performed in restricted areas only and should be used only upon the direction of the supervisor.

ADDITIONAL EQUIPMENT:

Nylon stripping pad (coarse, aggressive, loosely woven)

Aerosol dry stripping agent

Spray attachment unit

- - - - - - - - - - - - - - -

SAFETY PRECAUTIONS:

1. Do not discard aerosol cans with regular trash.

PROCEDURE:

1. Assemble equipment. Attach spray unit to floor machine. Prepare mopping solution.

2. Prepare area—move furniture, unplug electric appliances and equipment.

3. Sweep or dust floor with covered broom or floor tool. Pick up debris and discard.

MAINTENANCE OF FLOORS

PROCEDURE

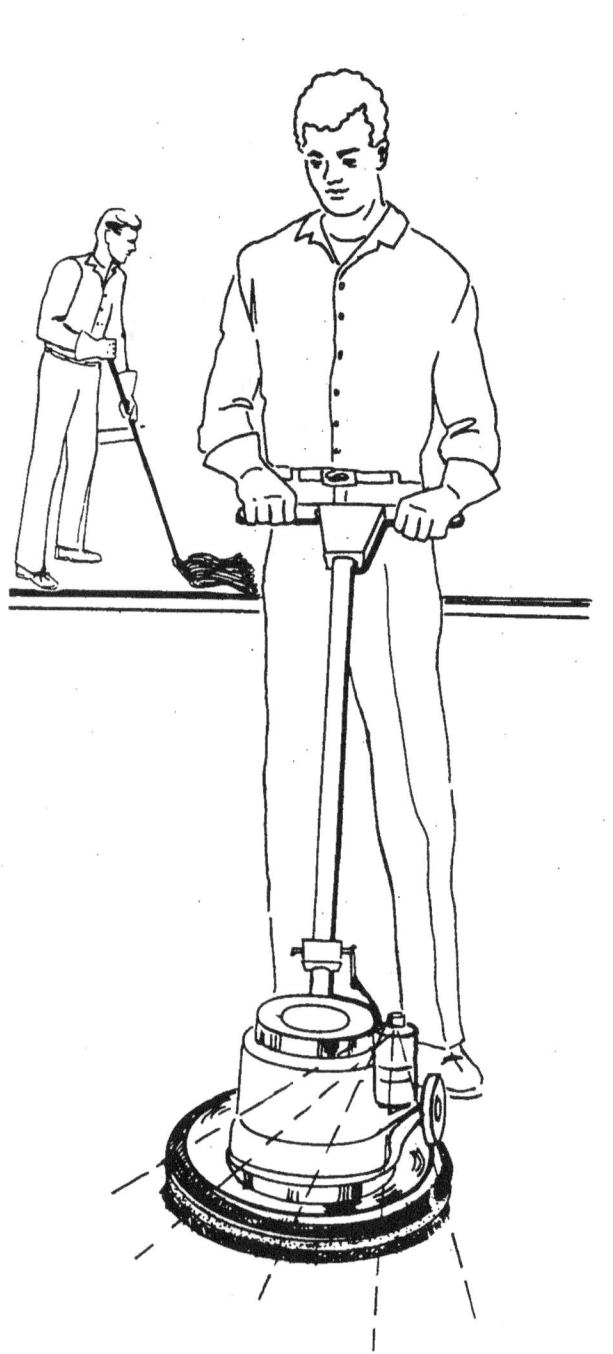

4. Dip mop into cleaning solution. Wring out thoroughly.

5. Damp mop area.

6. Shake aerosol stripping agent.

7. Snap can into spray unit. Keep dot on valve rim pointed down.

8. Apply stripping agent to floor (only enough for complete pad spread).
   a. Move machine *forward* and spread foam on first pass.

   b. Slowly move machine back over the same area to strip on second pass.

   c. Slowly move machine back over same area to burnish dry on third pass.

   d. Slowly move machine over same area on the fourth pass, applying stripping agent to new area—completing the four-step operation of the dry stripping system. (If the area is not dry on fourth pass, too much stripping agent was used.)

9. Move forward into next area. Overlap previous strokes and continue the four-step operation of spreading, stripping, and burnishing until area is completed.

10. Dust floor. Use *untreated* covered broom or floor tool. Pick up soil.

11. Dip mop into rinse water. Wring out thoroughly.

12. Damp mop area.

13. Apply floor finish as normally required.

MAINTENANCE OF FLOORS

PROCEDURE

---

14. Wash nylon pad immediately. Wash and dry all equipment and return to designated storage area.

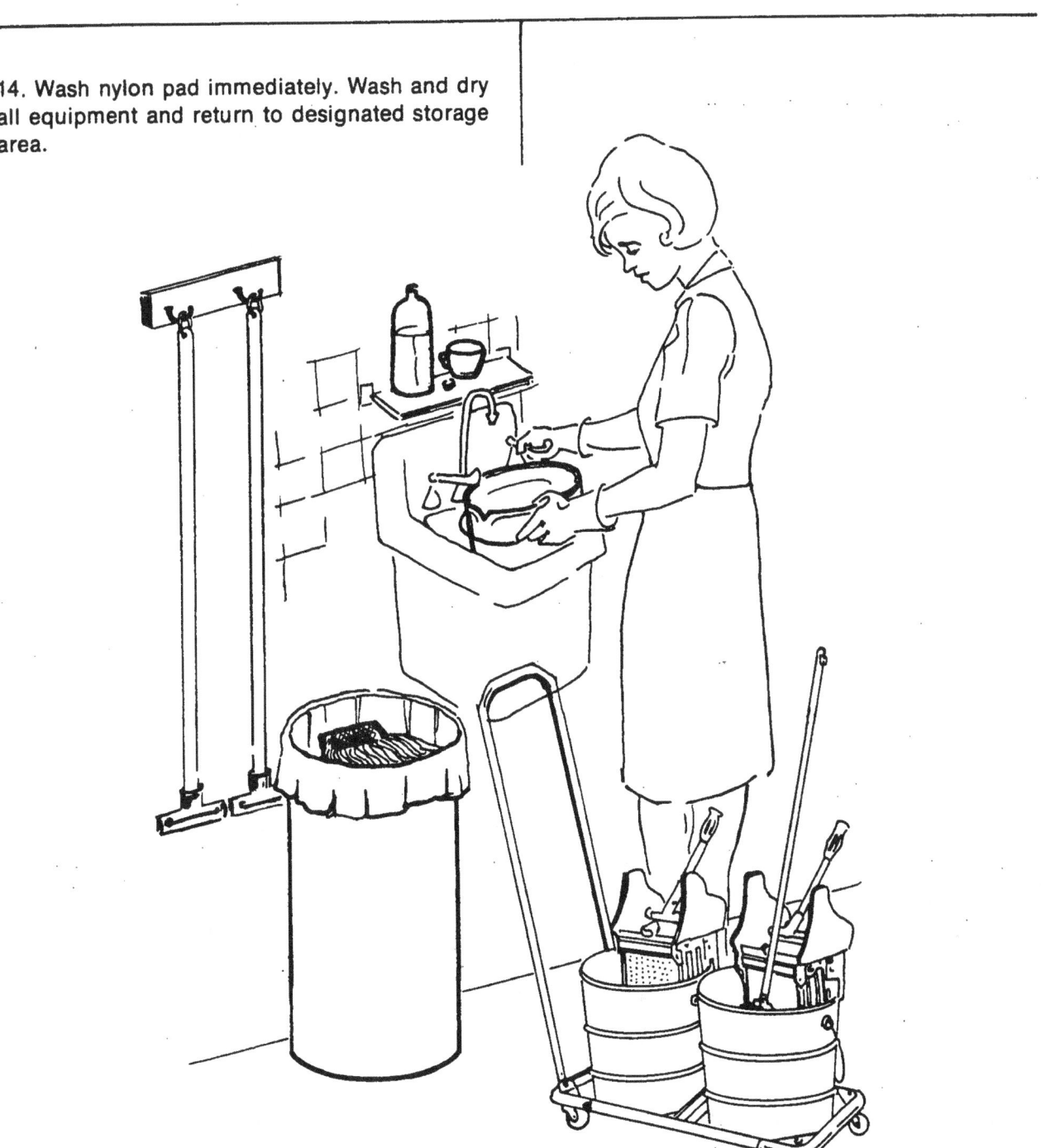

FINISHING FLOORS
(Sealers and Floor Finishes)

PURPOSE: To fill pores and cracks, prevent stains and deterioration, to provide protective coating and leveling to surface, to reduce maintenance, and to restore floors to their original finish.

EQUIPMENT:

    Synthetic sealer
    Synthetic Finish
    Electric floor machine
    Plastic liners
    Buckets and Wringers on dolly (two)
    Mopheads and handles (two)
    Cloths

SAFETY PRECAUTIONS:

1. Do not save contaminated/soiled solution. Discard.

2. Never pour any part of the used solution back into the container.

3. Never pour or drip finish on floor.

4. Remove spills and splashes of sealer or finish immediately. If allowed to dry, will not be able to remove.

PROCEDURE

1. Assemble equipment. Place plastic liners in buckets. Fold over rim and under handle. Take to assigned area.

2. Place mophead into one bucket. Pour sealer on mophead. Wring out mophead. Continue pouring small amounts of sealer onto mophead and wringing out until mophead is saturated. (This eliminates the waste of product.) Wring out. (Make sure mop does not drip.)

3. Apply two thin coats of sealer to floor surface. Apply first coat crosswise, and apply second coat lengthwise for complete coverage. Allow time for complete drying between coats.

4. Place second mophead into second bucket. Pour floor finish on mophead. Wring out mophead. Continue pouring small amounts of finish

MAINTENANCE OF FLOORS

PROCEDURE

onto mophead and wringing out until mophead is saturated. Wring out.

5. Apply three thin coats of floor finish to surface. Apply first coat crosswise, second coat lengthwise, and third coat crosswise for complete coverage and surface leveling. Whenver mop pulls or drags during application, return to solution. Allow time for complete drying between coats.

6. To make surface very hard and level/smooth, buff with polishing pad after each application, or complete the procedure, and buff floor after one hour drying time. (Do not use brush—will remove finish.)

BE CERTAIN THAT YOU:

Take equipment to utility room. Wash thoroughly. Place mophead into plastic liner/bag and place in laundry bag. Return equipment to designated storage area.

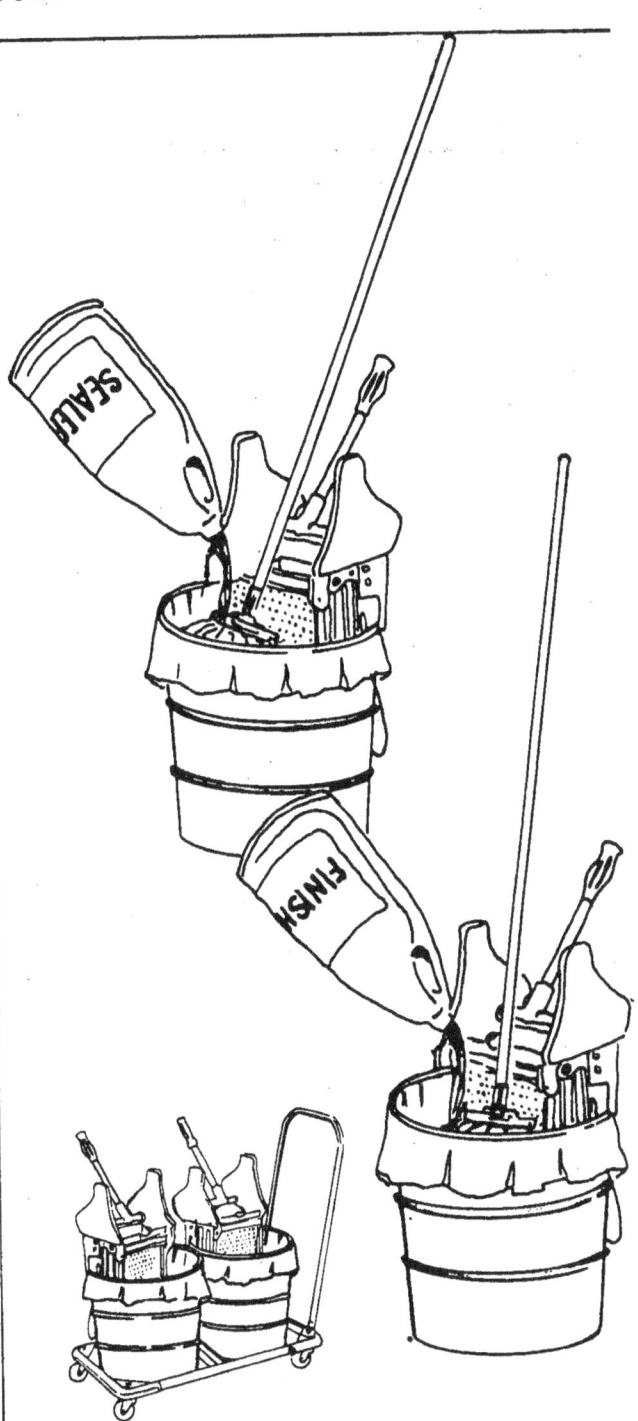

SPRAY BUFFING

PURPOSE: To maintain floor to optimum level. Also good for patching floors before they reach the point of needing a major refinishing job. Spray buffing is the basic method for maintaining resilient floors.

EQUIPMENT:

    Electric floor machine
    Aerosol cleaning agent, or
    Synthetic floor finish
    Nylon Pads (thick, loosely woven, aggressive)
    Sweeping tool
    Spray attachment unit, or
    Hand spray
    Brush with pad holder attachment, or
    Driving pad assembly
    Dustpan and Counter brush

SAFETY PRECAUTIONS:

    Same as for general buffing.

PROCEDURE

1. Assemble equipment. Attach spray unit to floor machine. Take to designated area.

2. Move furniture.

3. Sweep floor with covered floor tool. Pick up soil.

4. Shake aerosol cleaning agent. Snap can into spray unit.

5. Move floor machine to area, begin buffing as usual.

6. When black marks, spots, soil scuffs or scratches appear in the path of the buffer, spray a light mist on the areas. (If spray bottle is used, spray finish upward into air so that it falls to the floor in a mist instead of a stream.)

7. Buff same area until soil/damage is removed and shine appears. The machine will move

MAINTENANCE OF FLOORS

PROCEDURE

freely at first, then the area will become tacky or sticky before the shine appears.

8. Continue this procedure until area is repaired/clean. If area is too damaged, light scrub the area and apply thin coats of finish.

9. Remove pad or brush. Place in plastic liner. This procedure keeps pads/brushes moisted and makes cleaning easier.

10. Take equipment to utility room. Wash pads and place on flat surface or hang on peg to dry. Wipe off equipment and return to designated storage area.

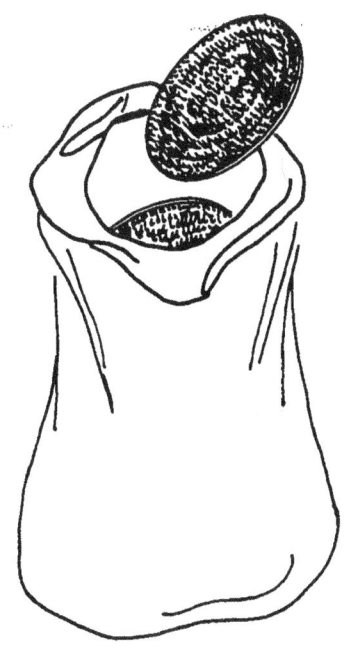

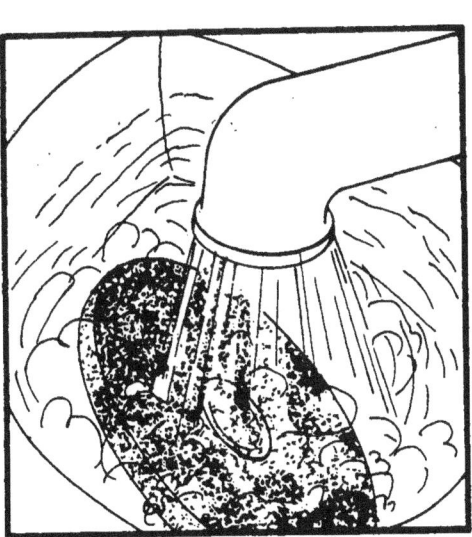

CARPET CARE
Cleaning and Spot Removal

PURPOSE: To remove dust, dirt, and grit particles, control bacteria, extend the life of the carpet and for appearance.

EQUIPMENT:

    Suction vacuum cleaner (Pile-lifting, upright machine with a brush and beater bar)
    White nylon hand brush with handle
    Shampooing machine
    Bucket and funnel
    Plastic boots or liners
    Wet and dry vacuum cleaner
    Shampooing agent
    Spot removing kit

SAFETY PRECAUTIONS:

1. Damp floors and uncleaned spills cause rot and mildew. Therefore, avoid soaking the carpet.

2. The steps to carpet care are:

    a. Vacuum

    b. Shampoo

    c. Remove spot

    d. Vacuum. Do not take any short cuts.

3. Release pressure in solution tank before removing cap.

4. Never wear shoes with dyed soles.

5. Protect carpet from rust stains. Use aluminum foil, cardboard, or plastic furniture coasters under legs of furniture.

PROCEDURE

1. Assemble equipment. Prepare solution. Pour into shampoo tank. Replace cap. Take to assigned area.

2. Move furniture. (If furniture cannot be moved out of area, move furniture to center of room. Vacuum, shampoo, remove spots, and vacuum perimeter. Replace furniture. Clean center of area/room.)

3. Vacuum with upright heavy duty pile lifting machine. Use three straight back-and-forth motions over the same area. (To prepare carpet for shampooing with regular vacuum, six back-and-forth strokes are required.)

MAINTENANCE OF FLOORS

23

PROCEDURE

---

4. Continue this procedure until entire carpet is vacuumed.

5. Shampoo carpet. Start in far corner of the room and work toward door. Set pile selector. Build up foam, and wait until foam appears around head of shampooing machine.

6. Take hand brush and shampoo along wall edges and corners.

7. Move machine in a forward and backward, or push and pull motion. Work across carpet, overlap each stroke.

8. Drop down to next area—overlap previous area. Continue procedure until carpet is completed.

9. If foam is brownish, vacuum immediately with wet vacuum; repeat shampooing procedure.

10. Remove any remaining spots.

11. Allow to dry.

12. Vacuuming *is a must in order to remove soil.*

13. Raise the pile with brush or machine.

14. Replace furniture. Aluminum foil, cardboard, or plastic furniture coasters may be placed under legs of furniture to avoid rust stains.

15. Take equipment to utility room. Clean. Hose off brush, wheels, and underneath shampoo machine. Wipe off exterior cabinet, and dry. Empty wet and dry vacuum. Wash and dry. Wash brush. Return all equipment to designated storage area.

USE AND CARE OF EQUIPMENT, MATERIALS, AND SUPPLIES

TABLE OF CONTENTS

		Page
I.	GENERAL POINTS TO BE OBSERVED	1
II.	USE AND CARE OF NON-AUTOMATIC/MANUAL EQUIPMENT	3
III.	USE AND CARE OF AUTOMATIC EQUIPMENT	8
IV.	HELPFUL SERVICE HINTS FOR WET AND DRY VACUUM	11
V.	HELPFUL SERVICE HINTS FOR FLOOR MACHINES	13
VI.	HELPFUL SERVICE HINTS FOR AUTOMATIC SCRUBBERS	14

USE AND CARE OF EQUIPMENT, MATERIALS, AND SUPPLIES

I. GENERAL POINTS TO BE OBSERVED

The institution has invested a large amount of money in expensive modern equipment, materials, and supplies in order to help fulfill the housekeeping goals. Therefore, it is the responsibility of each employee to keep the equipment in good working condition and use materials and supplies economically.

Storing of equipment is part of the housekeeping aid's job in caring for equipment. Some institutions have storage areas or utility rooms located in each department or on each floor. Others have central equipment rooms near the housekeeper's office. These areas are equipped with hooks, racks, shelves, sinks, and floor drains for the cleaning and storing of equipment, materials, and supplies.

The storage area must be maintained daily and every item must have a place.

Care of equipment, materials, and supplies are divided into two groups: care of non-automatic/manual equipment, and care of power-operated (electric or battery) equipment. However, there are several general points to be observed on the care and upkeep of all equipment, materials, and supplies.

1. Follow manufacturer's instructions for operation and maintenance.

2. Provide a preventive maintenance program (routine and systematic inspections and repairs).

3. Replace equipment, materials, or supplies promptly when faulty or ineffective.

4. Keep equipment clean at all times.

5. Use materials and supplies economically.

6. Provide adequate and proper storage area for equipment, materials, and supplies.

7. Use each piece of equipment only for its intended purpose.

8. Report faulty, damaged, or ineffective materials or equipment to the supervisor.

PURPOSE: To maintain equipment in good working condition; to insure faster, easier, and more efficient performance; to control bacteria and for appearance.

EQUIPMENT:
    Germicidal detergent
    Cloths or sponges
    Buckets (two)
    Gloves

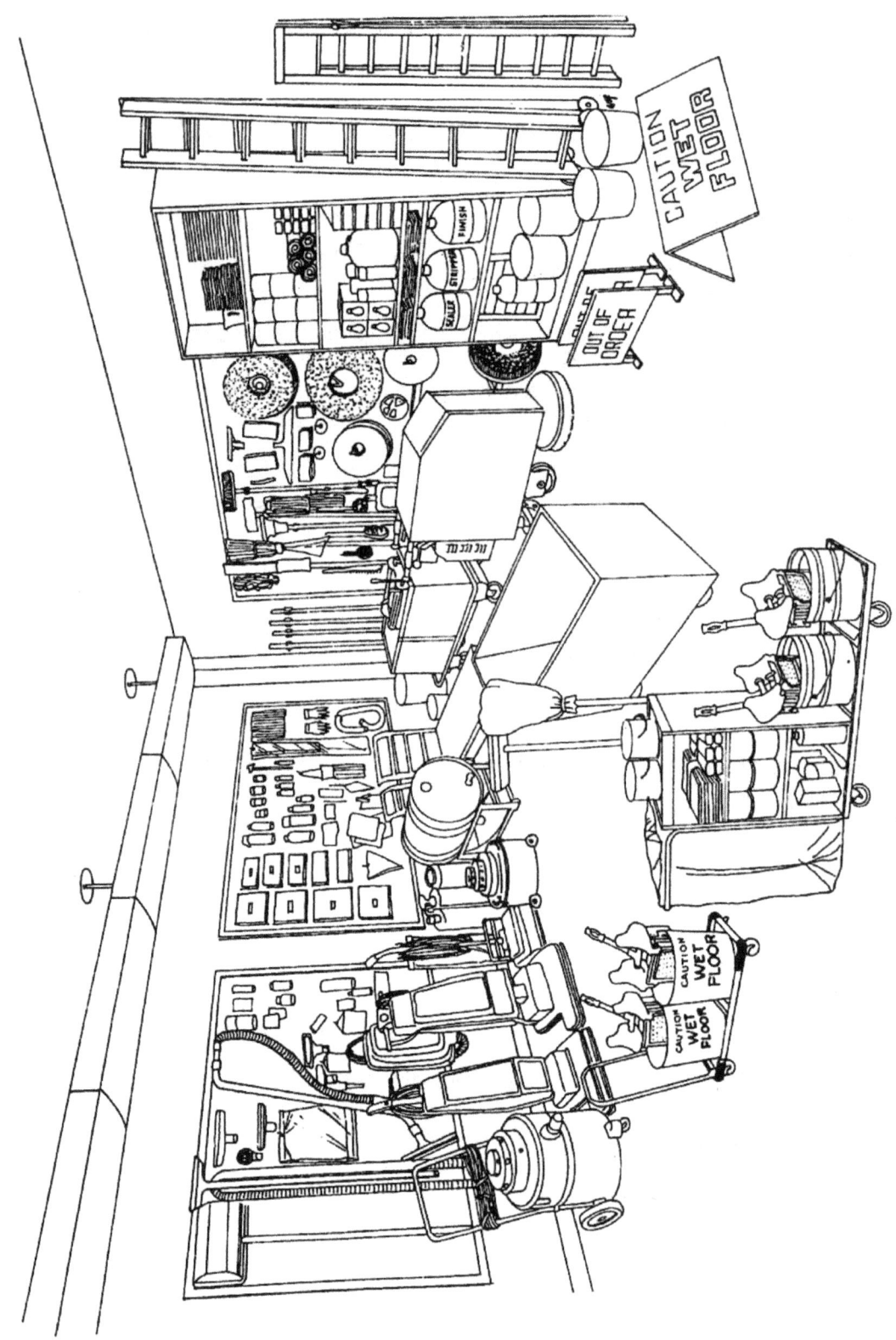

SAFETY PRECAUTIONS:

1. Never pour used sealer or finish back into clean solution containers.

2. Brushes should never be stored on the bristles or left on machines.

3. Do not use more of an item than is necessary to efficiently perform the task.

4. Make sure pressure is released from wall washing tanks before cleaning.

5. All equipment must be cleaned at the end of the day and returned to designated storage area.

II. USE AND CARE OF NON-AUTOMATIC/MANUAL EQUIPMENT

Included in this type of equipment are items used in housekeeping duties that are entirely moved or operated by hand. This includes everything from brushes to wall washing pressure tanks.

EQUIPMENT:
- Utility carts
- Brushes of all types:
    a. Counter
    b. Sweeping
    c. Toilet
    d. Deck and other scrub brushes
    e. Radiator
    f. Scrub and polish
    g. Pot
    h. Nylon hand brush
    i. Coving or baseboard
- Dustpans
- Screens, sifters, and slit spoons
- Caution signs
- Squeegees
- Buckets (small and large)
- Dollies
- Wringers
- Mopheads
- Nylon pads
- Sweeping floor tools
- Extension handles
- Trash carts
- Wall washing pressure tanks
- Ladders
- Gloves
- Sealers
- Strippers (bulk and portioned)
- Finishes (bulk and portioned)
- Germicidal detergents (bulk and portioned)
- Polishes (furniture, stainless steel)
- Treated cloths
- Dust cloths
- Soaps
- Plastic liners
- Carpet sweepers
- Putty knives
- Hose (water)
- Measuring cups
- Mopping tanks
- Spray units
- Toilet tissue
- Paper towels
- Bottles (plastic)
- Trash containers
- Corn brooms

4

PROCEDURE

Utility Carts

1. Wipe off all shelves with germicidal cloth at the end of the day. Dry.
2. Place plastic liner on top shelf to keep from rusting.
3. Use it daily in performing duties as assigned.
4. Keep shelves neatly stocked with all supplies and equipment.

Brushes

1. Clean at the end of the day.
2. Comb with a stiff fiber brush or comb and wash under running water. Shake out excess water.
3. Store by hanging on rack, free from touching any surface or store on block/wood part of the brush.
4. Do not use until bristles are dry.
5. For maximum wear and effectiveness, brushes with removable handles should be rotated at least once a week.
6. Always hang broom up. Never stand on the straws.

Bottles (Plastic Spray Bottle)

1. Clean exterior with paper towel dipped in germicidal solution. Dry.
2. Return to utility cart.
3. A trigger type must be taken apart regularly and washed and rinsed thoroughly.

Carpet Sweepers

1. Empty into plastic liner after each use. Place liner in trash collection container.
2. Remove strings and debris from brush and wheel.
3. Damp wipe the sweeper.

Caution Signs (Wet Floor, Out of Order)

1. Damp wipe and dry after each use.
2. Periodically, thoroughly wash, rinse, and dry.

Cloths (Treated and Cleaning)

1. Treated
    a. Use all surfaces of the woven treated paper before discarding.
    b. Treat own cloths by spraying lightly with solution and allow to stand overnight in covered container. May be discarded or laundered.
2. Cleaning:
    a. Rinse frequently during use.
    b. At the end of the day or at the end of the bathroom cleaning procedure, place cleaning cloths in plastic liner, then put into a regular laundry bag for laundering.
    c. Never leave cloths lying around.

Dustpans

1. Clean at the end of the day. Wash with germicidal solution.
2. Rinse and dry.
3. Hang on hook on cart so that it will not become bent or damaged.

Extension Handles

1. Use as an aid for high dusting.
2. Wipe off daily.

Floor Sweeping Tools

1. Use a disposable cloth.
2. Use all surfaces possible.
3. Damp wipe handle and foot frame daily.
4. Wash tool once a week with germicidal detergent.
5. Hang up on utility cart when not in use.

Germicidal Detergents and Strippers

1. Used in the cleaning operation to remove soil.
2. Do not overuse—will destroy flooring surfaces.
3. Use recommended amount only.
4. Read label before using.

Gloves

1. Wash outside of gloves under running water (while on hand) at the end of the day.
2. Remove and wash inside. Wipe dry.
3. Hang across a smooth surface to dry.

Hose (With Cut-off Nozzle)

1. Rinse off rubber or plastic hose.
2. Roll in a three-foot circle to prevent kinking. Drain water while rolling.
3. Hang hose on a rack or peg in storage area.

Knives (Putty—Short and Long)

1. Wipe handle and blade with germicidal solution at end of day. Dry.
2. Return to cart.

Ladders (Safety and Platform)

1. Wipe off after each use with germicidal solution.
2. Rinse and dry.
3. Return to designated storage area.

Measuring Cups

1. Rinse immediately after use.
2. Dry.
3. Store so that it will not be damaged.

Mops—Dust

1. Do not use to mop up spills.
2. Remove loose soil from mop frequently, by vacuum if possible.
3. Remove mophead at end of day, place in plastic bag and take to designated storage area for laundering.

Mops—Wet

1. Cut off loose and uneven yarn strands.
2. Never twist or squeeze mop extra hard; such action will break fibers and destroy the mophead.
3. Remove mophead at the end of bathroom cleaning and at the end of the day.
4. Place in plastic bag and into laundry bag and take to designated storage area for laundering.

Mopping Tanks, Buckets, Wringers, and Dollies

1. Remove any loose mophead yarn, string, or foreign matter.
2. Wash, rinse, and dry daily. Invert small and medium size buckets to dry.
3. Keep the equipment in good repair. Report any defects to supervisor.
4. When necessary, add a few drops of oil to casters.
5. Avoid hitting the mopping unit against other objects and walls.
6. Replace bumper strip when needed.
7. Do not allow a cleaning solution to remain in the bucket when the bucket is not in use.

Small Buckets or Pails

1. Empty contents.
2. Wash, rinse, and dry.
3. Turn upside down to dry.

Polishes

1. Used on furniture, stainless steel, wood, and metal.
2. Use only the recommended amount.
3. It is very annoying to get polish on one's clothes, so thoroughly rub the surface to remove excess polish.

Paper Towels and Toilet Tissue

1. Replacement supplies.
2. Always place in containers, not in window sills or on top of cabinets.

Screens, Sifters/Slit Spoons

1. Wash and shake off excess water.
2. Dry. Handle so as not to bend screen.
3. Place on hook on utility cart or other designated storage area.

Nylon Pads

1. Wash pads under running water. Rinse.
2. Hang or store on flat surface until dry.

Plastic Liners

1. Used to line trash containers.
2. Must be replaced daily.
3. Do not use for any other purpose than intended.

Sealers, Finishers

1. Items used to protect flooring.
2. These items are very expensive.
3. Use liners in buckets when using sealer and finish.
4. Never pour solution on floor.
5. Wipe up spills or drips immediately.
6. Never waste the product. Pour just enough on mophead in bucket to wet mophead, which should eliminate any material being left over.
7. In case there is a small amount left over, discard it. Do not pour into clean solution; solution will sour.
8. Mopheads should be placed in plastic liner/bag for laundering.
9. Wash, rinse, and dry buckets, wringers, dolly, mops, and mop handles used in these operations.

Soaps

1. Used for hand washing and bathing.
2. Must rinse before using.
3. Not used for cleaning inanimate surfaces.

Sponges

1. Place in germicidal solution. Wash thoroughly. Squeeze out excess water.
2. Rinse. Squeeze out excess water.
3. Place on flat surface to dry. Do not hang on nails.

Squeegees (Small or Large)

1. Wash squeegee blades in germicidal solution.
2. Rinse. Drain off excess water.
3. Wipe dry and return to utility cart or storage area.
4. Do not store with squeegee blades down.

Spray Units

1. Used for spray buffing and dry stripping.
2. Wipe off with germicidal solution.
3. Rinse spray nozzles.
4. Do not let material harden on nozzle.

Trash Containers

1. Used to receive or hold waste.
2. Handle containers so as not to scratch, puncture, or bend them.
3. Wipe trash container inside and out daily. Replace liner.
4. Once a month, collect trash containers, take to utility room, and thoroughly wash, rinse, and dry or steam clean.

Trash Carts

1. Used for general collection of trash.
2. Take to utility room. Wash inside and outside thoroughly. Let drain.
3. Rinse and let drain.
4. Wipe dry.

Wall Washing Machines/Pressure Tanks

1. Empty at the end of the operation.
2. Rinse tubing and inside of tanks.
3. Wipe off outside with germicidal detergent. Dry.
4. Store in designated storage area.

III. USE AND CARE OF AUTOMATIC EQUIPMENT

Automatic equipment is equipment that is power operated either by electricity or battery. This type of equipment is very expensive and must be properly maintained to insure good service and maximum efficiency. Therefore, keep this equipment free of dirt, and oiled properly, and keep screws and nuts tight. Automatic equipment is usually divided into three categories: floor machines, vacuum cleaners, and automatic scrubbers.

EQUIPMENT:
    Single disc floor machines, with or without spray attachments
    Drive assemblies
    Square buffers—attachments (plates and baseboard scrubbers)
    Shampoo machines
    Vacuums
        a. Suction
        b. Back-Pack
        c. Wet and dry
        d. Pile lifter
        e. Upright

Vacuum attachments (wand, hose, crevice tool, brushes), floor, wall, ceiling, upholstery, carpet and attachments for wet floor operation.
Battery-operated sweepers
Automatic mop assemblies

PROCEDURE

Floor Machines

1. Used for scrubbing, stripping, and polishing of large or small areas quickly. Also used for special application, such as spray buffing and dry stripping.
2. Never attach brush by running machine over it and allowing it to lock.
3. Never leave machine unattended. Disconnect when not in use.
4. Machine is cleaned at the end of the day or after completion of assignment.

    a. At the work site, tilt machine back on handle. Remove brush and pad or drive assembly and place in plastic liners/bags.
    b. Rinse machine in upright position. Damp wipe cord with germicidal cloth. Wind cord on handle or storage hooks as it is being wiped. Inspect for defects and report to supervisor.
    c. Take equipment to utility room. Remove brushes, pads and/or drive assembly from plastic liners/bags. Wash thoroughly under running water. Store on flat surface or hang on peg to dry. DO NOT USE AGAIN UNTIL DRY.
    d. Wash handle and exterior surface of machine. Dry.
    e. Tilt on handle and rinse the underside of the brush housing with clean water. Dry.
    f. If a solution tank is used, rinse tank and feed lines/tubing. Dry.
    g. Store equipment in designated storage area.
    h. Never store machines on brushes. Store in tilted position.

Extension Cords

1. If an extension cord is used, make sure it is the same size as on the equipment so that the proper amount of current is carried to machine.
2. Do not yank on an electric cord to pull the plug from the outlet.
3. Damp wipe cord with germicidal solution. Dry.
4. Wind loosely and hang or lay in a safe place.

Vacuum Cleaners (Upright, Wet and Dry, Back-Pack)

1. Used to remove soil from floors and carpeting, window sills, ledges, screens, vents, blinds, upholstery, walls, and ceiling; and to pick up water—scrub, rinse, overflow, flooding.
2. Empty upright vacuums when bag is half full
    a. Outer bags may be cloth, moleskin, or paper.
    b. Cloth and moleskin bags may be vacuumed, but never washed. Discard disposable bags.
    c. Damp wipe handle, hose, and cord with germicidal solution. Dry.

3. Clean wet and dry vacuum at the end of the day.
    a. If used for dry purposes:
        (1) Make sure machine is set up with flannel and paper liners.

(2) To clean, remove hose, head assembly, and cloth filter. Leave paper filter in place.
(3) Tilt machine back on handle and wheels. Pull out bag so that it hangs outward.
(4) Continue raising machine until it is resting on handle. Slap tank several times to dislodge all dirt.
(5) Remove bag by sliding elastic band off the lip of the tank. Place in a plastic liner. Tie and discard.
(6) Wash tank inside and outside with germicidal solution. Rinse and dry.
(7) Wash all attachments. Rinse and dry.
(8) Wipe off cord and rewind on handle, not around head assembly.
(9) Wipe off head assembly.
(10) Check impaction filter. Not necessary to remove after each usage, unless torn, damaged or wet. Supervisor should set a specific time for changing (for example, every 30 days).
(11) Take equipment to designated storage area. Leave head assembly off tank. Turn on side for airing and drying purposes.

b. If used for wet purposes:
(1) Make sure machine is set up for the wet operation.
(2) Remove flannel and paper liners and insert the cyclonic separator which has a float that shuts off the suction of the machine when tank is filled to maximum level.
(3) To clean, remove hose, head assembly, and lift out cyclonic separator.
(4) Wheel machine to area with drain or low sink. Tilt back on handles to empty. (Some of these have drain valves.)
(5) Rinse two or three times with clean water to remove sludge.
(6) Wash, rinse, and dry tank and accessories.
(7) Store in designated storage area.
(8) If impaction filter is wet, allow to dry. Sterilize or autoclave before using again.

Automatic Scrubbers/Sweepers

Used for scrubbing, stripping, buffing, and sweeping large areas. In order for machines to work properly, they must be charged daily in a well-ventilated room. Battery must be checked regularly and distilled water added when water is below internal plate or triangle. Battery cover must be left opened when charging. Do not smoke in area when machine is being charged.

1. Automatic Scrubber
   a. To clean, take equipment to utility room. Empty; open dump valve or fold tanks over drain.
   b. Flush tanks, wheels, and squeegee. Use a hose to perform this task.
   c. Wash exterior surface with germicidal solution.
   d. Rinse and dry.
   e. Take to designated storage area.
   f. Make sure windows are open.
   g. Report any defects, damages, or necessary repairs to supervisor.

2. Powered Sweeper
   a. To clean, take to utility room. Remove and empty trash pan.
   b. Shake down filters; remove and empty pan.

c. Remove brushes; comb, wash, rinse, and shake well. Dry.
d. Wash exterior surface with germicidal solution. Rinse and dry.
e. Wash pans. Rinse and dry.
f. Replace all parts.
g. Take to designated storage area.
h. Check battery; leave cover open.
i. Connect for charging.
j. Make sure windows are open.
k. Report any defects or necessary repairs to supervisor

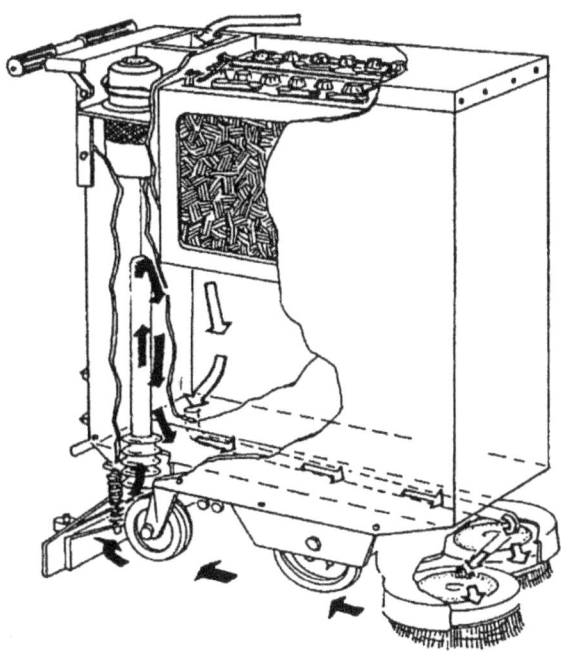
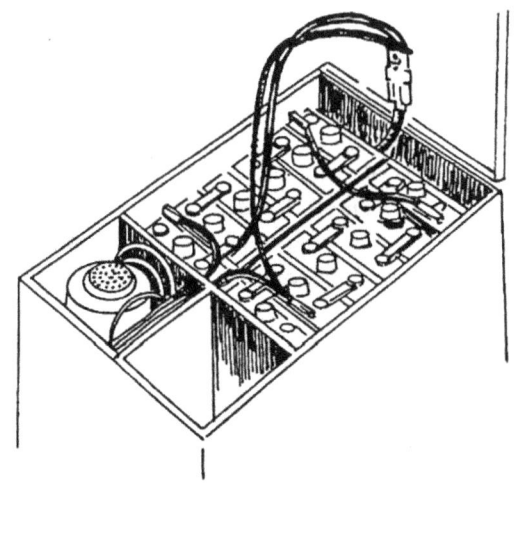

IV. HELPFUL SERVICE HINTS FOR WET AND DRY VACUUM

1. Always operate vacuum on the proper voltages as outlined on the data plate.

2. After using for dry applications, remove the disposable paper bag (5 to 9 gallon units only), and mitten flannel filter and clean before reusing. For added convenience, keep a supply of disposable paper bags on hand (5 and 9 gallon units only; they may be obtained from your authorized distributor.

3. If air movement is interrupted in your vacuum, check the dust filter to make sure it's clean. To see if hose has become clogged, remove hose from machine and test suction at machine intake. Sometimes a clogged tool will be the culprit, so check tools periodically.

4. For wet work, remove the disposable paper bag and dust filter, then place the water separator in the tank (5 and 9 gallon units only). In the 10 gallon models, install the wet filter and water shut-off.

5. After using machine for wet work, and before putting it away, clean tank inside and outside; clean tools thoroughly.

6. Store machinery in clean dry place.

7. The suds suppressor bar at the tank inlet should be checked and replaced, if necessary, after 125 gallons of solution have been picked up. Suds suppressor bar is replaced by removing inlet deflector and sliding new bar into place. These bars may be obtained from authorized distributor (for 5 and 9 gallon units only).

8. Many tools are available for the wet and dry vacuum. Contact your authorized distributor for additional tools.

SERVICE DIAGNOSIS:

1. Motor will not start
   a. Possible causes:
      (1) Power source or outlet dead
      (2) Vacuum switch faulty or damaged
      (3) Excessively worn brushes
      (4) Wire shorted or broken

   b. How to correct:
      (1) Activate source or check cord
      (2) Replace switch
      (3) Replace brushes
      (4) Replace wires

2. Little or no suction
   a. Possible causes:
      (1) Full tank; wet shut-off closes fan inlet
      (2) Clogged attachment inlet, hose or vacuum inlet
      (3) Clogged filter bag
      (4) Tank gasket seal leaks
      (5) Exhaust air outlet covered

   b. How to correct:
      (1) Empty tank
      (2) Remove lodged materials
      (3) Clean filter bag
      (4) Position seal properly
      (5) Remove obstruction

3. Machine noisy
   a. Possible causes:
      (1) Vibration or resonating of metal parts
      (2) Dirty filter

    b. How to correct:
        (1) Secure all mountings firmly
        (2) Clean filter

4. Motor runs hot or smells warm
    a. Possible causes:
        (1) Motor cooling air intake or exhaust clogged
        (2) Motor overloaded with mist or suds
        (3) Dirty filter

    b. How to correct:
        (1) Clean air intake and exhaust passages
        (2) Empty tank; install new suds suppressor
        (3) Clean filter

V. HELPFUL SERVICE HINTS FOR FLOOR MACHINES

SERVICE DIAGNOSIS:

1. Machine wobbles; hard to control
    a. Possible causes:
        (1) Brush bristles distorted resulting in brush being uneven
        (2) Switch housing not tight on handle tube
        (3) Handle tube not connected firmly to machine hose
        (4) Pads or brushes worn unevenly

    b. How to correct:
        (1) If brush is new, soak in water for several hours; remove from water; shake off excess water; rest brush on flat surface on back with bristles pointing upward.
        (2) Tighten bolts securing housing to handle tube; tighten set screws. If housing is still loose, drill and tap new hole in housing, insert pointed set screw and tighten firmly.
        (3) Check all mounting bolts for tightness; insert washers for shims if necessary.
        (4) Replace with new pad or brush.

2. Motor will not run
    a. Possible causes:
        (1) Unplugged at wall
        (2) Unplugged between motor and handle cable.
        (3) Fuse blown or circuit breaker tripped
        (4) Cable wires severed
        (5) Switch burned out
        (6) Wires detached at switch
        (7) Motor burned out

    b. How to correct; follow these steps:
        (1) Visibly check all connections to be sure the plugs are securely plugged into the appropriate receptacle.
        (2) Check fuse or circuit breaker. Replace or reset if necessary.

(3) Visibly and carefully check cable for wire breakage.
(4) Unplug motor from handle cable and connect motor directly to wall receptacle through use of an adequate gauge extension cord (at least 14-2). CAUTION: Remove brush or pad holder from machine before plugging into power source.
(5) If after #4 above motor does not operate, remove motor from machine and take it to your distributor, or an electrical repair station designated by your distributor for repairs.
(6) If after #4 above does operate, the problem lies between the motor and the wall receptacle. Remove switch box cover plate and ascertain that al electrical connections are secure.
(7) Remove cable from the terminals on the switch and replace with an extension cord (preferably 14-3) to determine if wires have been severed inside the cable.
(8) Replace switch.

3. Runs hot
   a. Possible causes:
   (1) Motor overloaded. Machine does not have sufficient power for the job. (Example: dry spray-buff cleaning with abrasive pad.)
   (2) Air intake ducts clogged with dust and lint.

   b. How to correct:
   (1) Secure the proper machine for the job or use the same machine with pads of less abrasive material.
   (2) Remove drip cover and shroud. Use forced air to blow dust and lint from motor.

VI. HELPFUL SERVICE HINTS FOR AUTOMATIC SCRUBBERS

SERVICE DIAGNOSIS:

1. Motor will not start
   a. Possible causes:
   (1) Battery charge condition very low; check with hydrometer
   (2) Battery connectors loose or disconnected
   (3) Loose or broken wires

   b. How to correct:
   (1) Recharge batteries fully before beginning operations
   (2) Fasten battery connections securely
   (3) Fasten all wires securely and tape

2. Machine will not move
   a. Possible causes:
   (1) Clutch requires adjusting
   (2) "V" belt slipping
   (3) Battery charge condition very low; check with hydrometer

    b. How to correct:
       (1) Adjust clutch per "Clutch Adjustment" instructions
       (2) Adjust "V" belt tightness
       (3) Recharge batteries fully before beginning operations

3. Machine streaking a cleaned floor
    a. Possible causes:
       (1) Foreign materials lodged under rear squeegee blade
       (2) Insufficient water flow to brushes
       (3) Worn squeegee blades
       (4) Squeegee out of adjustment
       (5) Worn brushes or pads

    b. How to correct:
       (1) Raise squeegee and clean squeegee blade
       (2) Clean fine filter screen in tank and examine lines for a flow restriction
       (3) Replace squeegee blade
       (4) Adjust per instructions
       (5) Replace brushes or pads

4. Solution not being properly picked up
    a. Possible causes:
       (1) Vacuum motor wired for 12 or 18 volts and too much solution being laid
       (2) Clogged pick-up tube
       (3) Air leaks around vacuum motor mount
       (4) Ball check (water shut-off) sealing vacuum motor opening to tank
       (5) Clogged filters
       (6) Drain valve not completely closed
       (7) Pick-up tube plug or suds suppressors not seated properly

    b. How to correct:
       (1) Use 24-volt switch position
       (2) Remove lint accumulations and clean tube through plugged hole in tank at top of tube
       (3) Seal all leaks
       (4) Clean ball check (water shut-off) assembly
       (5) Replace filters
       (6) Close valve
       (7) Securely seat pick-up tube plug

5. Short operating time
    a. Possible causes:
       (1) Battery charge condition very low; check with hydrometer
       (2) Continuous heavy motor load due to special brushes
       (3) Constant brush operation; 210 lb. position

    b. How to correct:
       (1) Recharge batteries fully before beginning operations
       (2) Use special brushes requiring heavy motor load only for particular application
       (3) Use locked brush cleaning operations sparingly

6. Machine pulls to one side
   a. Possible causes
      (1) Squeegee dragging only on one side

   b. How to correct:
      (1) Adjust per instructions

7. Machine creeps
   a. Possible causes:
      (1) Clutch out of proper adjustment
      (2) Clutch cable binding in wound wire casing
      (3) Clutch collar sticking

   b. How to correct:
      (1) Adjust clutch per "Clutch Adjustment" instructions
      (2) Lubricate clutch cable and casing
      (3) Lubricate clutch

www.ingramcontent.com/pod-product-compliance
Lightning Source LLC
Chambersburg PA
CBHW080325020526
44117CB00035B/2653